# We Did Nothing

Linda Polman studied at the Utrecht School of Journalism. For the last twenty years she has been a freelance journalist for Dutch radio, television and newspapers. Since the publication of her book in Holland, Polman has lectured to government, military and academic audiences throughout the region. An earlier translation of the full story of Kibeho was first published in *Granta* magazine. Polman currently divides her time between West Africa and Holland.

# We Did Nothing

*Why the Truth Doesn't Always Come Out When the UN Goes In*

LINDA POLMAN

*Translated by Rob Bland*

VIKING
*an imprint of*
PENGUIN BOOKS

VIKING

Published by the Penguin Group
Penguin Books Ltd, 80 Strand, London WC2R ORL, England
Penguin Putnam Inc., 375 Hudson Street, New York, New York 10014, USA
Penguin Books Australia Ltd, 250 Camberwell Road, Camberwell, Victoria 3124, Australia
Penguin Books Canada Ltd, 10 Alcorn Avenue, Toronto, Ontario, Canada M4V 3B2
Penguin Books India (P) Ltd, 11 Community Centre,
Panchsheel Park, New Delhi – 110 017, India
Penguin Books (NZ) Ltd, Cnr Rosedale and Airborne Roads,
Albany, Auckland, New Zealand
Penguin Books (South Africa) (Pty) Ltd, 24 Sturdee Avenue,
Rosebank 2196, South Africa

Penguin Books Ltd, Registered Offices: 80 Strand, London WC2R ORL, England

www.penguin.com

Original edition published in Dutch under the title
'k Zag twee beren (I Saw Two Bears) by Atlas, Amsterdam 1997
Revised edition published in Dutch by Rozenberg Publishers, Amsterdam, 2002
Revised edition first published in English under the title We Did Nothing by Viking 2003
1

The publishers would like to thank the Foundation for the Production and Translation
of Dutch Literature and the Foundation for Journalistic Research Projects for their
financial support of this book

Set in 12/14.75pt Monotype Bembo
Typeset by Rowland Phototypesetting Ltd, Bury St Edmunds, Suffolk
Printed in Great Britain by Clays Ltd, St Ives plc

A CIP catalogue record for this book is available from the British Library

ISBN 0-670-91424-X

# Contents

# Preface

I wrote this book whilst covering the UN peacekeeping missions around the world throughout the 1990s. I travelled to Somalia, Haiti and Rwanda, witnessing how the world's most powerful countries manipulate the United Nations to fulfil their own national interests. In this book I describe what is happening in these 'peacekeeping zones' – the daily, sometimes absurd and often terrifying consequences of this manipulation for the UN peacekeeping soldiers who are sent to the frontline. They are the ones who must stand by and watch as the UN fiascos take shape.

In the late 1990s, I went to New York, to visit the enormous UN Headquarters on First Avenue. I was on an assignment to write about how the UN Member States go about their business in the UN, how they come by the resolutions that scatter those hapless UN soldiers around the world, and that we read about in our morning newspapers. An American diplomat whom I met outside the UN offices succinctly summarized the process I had witnessed inside the building: 'UN resolutions are like hotdogs. If you know how they make 'em, you don't want to eat 'em. You just swallow. No questions asked.'

Then 11 September 2001 happened. It is thought that the epic destruction of the World Trade Center on that day would change everything, including international politics. It didn't, or not as far as the UN Member States' pursuit of national agendas go. '9/11' has provided only one of many opportunities for this breathless pursuit to continue even as governments change and the threat of terrorism looms. Ten years ago, in his first speech to the UN's General Assembly in October 1993, former American President Bill Clinton announced that he was tired of the UN approving missions too complicated and extensive for the organization to accomplish. He was referring particularly to the UN peace mission in Somalia, with which America no longer wished to collaborate after eighteen American military had lost their lives. 'The UN should learn to say No,' was Clinton's advice, after which America walked out of Somalia.

Ten years later, as I write this in February 2003, Clinton's successor, President George W. Bush, is making it perfectly clear that in America's ongoing 'War on Terror', the US intends to do whatever it thinks is necessary, even if this means declaring war on Iraq. They will do this with UN approval if the Security Council agrees to support them. If the Security Council does not approve, they will do it anyway. Should the UN finally learn to say No? I hope this book might help us understand why the question is important.

Linda Polman, Sierra Leone, February 2003

# Prologue:
# Hotdogs in New York

## I

*New York, May 2000*

They have dug up the pavement in front of UN Headquarters. Blue UN tarpaulins, home to thousands of refugees in more than twenty of the world's disaster zones, here provide shade for New York construction workers. Lengths of sewer pipe litter the site. The UN's ground-floor toilets are leaking. Again. In their efforts to maintain international peace and security, the United Nations are assembled in a 39-storey office block that, in maintenance terms, is more like a squat. While outside the flags of the Member States flutter proudly in the breeze.

In the UN enclave along First Avenue, international law prevails, but beyond the railings surrounding UN HQ it is the New York City Police Department who run the show. The cops won't allow me to cross the street. Even UN diplomats are held back on the sidewalk.

'*Que pasa?*' inquires a diplomat from Member State Cuba, fishing a box of cigars from his inside pocket.

'*Cleengtong pasa,*' replies a cop with a smattering of Spanish. 'In New York for some fundraising quickie.'

More than 2,000 agents have been drafted in to shield Clinton from danger. At the far end of the Avenue we see hundreds of headlights appear. Then a fleet of flashing helicopters zooms into view. '*Como los Star Wars,*' mutters the

Cuban. Clinton's limo streaks past, a hand moving back and forth behind the smoked glass.

'*Gringo vanidosissimo*,' yells the Cuban, stabbing his cigar after the disappearing procession. American show-off.

On 26 June 1945, barely a month after the capitulation of Nazi Germany and while the Second World War was still raging in Asia, fifty-one countries from the allied coalition signed the United Nations Charter in San Francisco. The fifty-one, euphorically disposed, ranged themselves behind a two-fold objective: 'to save succeeding generations from the scourge of war, which twice in our lifetime has brought untold sorrow to mankind' and 'to promote social progress and better standards of life in larger freedom' for the population of the world.

Half a century later, and the number of Member States has almost quadrupled. The ambassadors of 191 governments are now the 'cast' who animate the tableau in the office building on the Hudson River. As the official representatives of 98 per cent of the world's 6 billion inhabitants, it is they who determine which of their national problems fall within the United Nations remit. On average they manage to cram 170 issues per year on to the General Assembly's agenda. El Niño, atomic energy and the removal of landmines. Palestine, East Timor and the Tamils. Decolonization and female circumcision. The law of the sea, international postal services, human rights. The island of Mayotte is demanding a hearing for its long struggle for independence from the rest of the Comoros. The United States is demanding yet another hearing on Iraq. Member States are also grappling with climate change and with international crime, not to mention internal UN appointments: judges for genocide tribunals and new non-permanent members of the Security Council.

A number of questions have become permanent fixtures on

the UN agenda, thanks to their insolubility: the Palestinian right to self-determination, fishing wars and the arms race (nuclear and biological) in space and on the ocean floor. Botswanans and Icelanders each have their own motives when casting their vote in the General Assembly. New Zealanders have quite other ideas about the right time for war and the right time for peace than the Nepalese. Nevertheless, the General Assembly is said to be one of the most admirable phenomena on the planet: 'A hundred and ninety-one voting members, representing every conceivable culture and religion, plumage, commitment and GNP, who every now and then agree with each other about something. I tell you: it's a bloody miracle,' says a British diplomat on his way into the chamber.

Of the UN's 191 Member States, 144 are rated poor countries. New York landlords are keenly aware of the fact. 'No pets. No UN diplomats' is the rule for many apartments. Of the 144, forty-eight are classified as LDCs, UN jargon for 'Least Developed Countries', the poorest of the world's poor. Madagascar is one of them. Outside the revolving doors I meet up with a fellow UN correspondent who works for a paper in Antananarivo, the capital of Madagascar I now discover. His entire print run would fit into a New York grocery bag, because only rich Madagascans can read. I ask him if today's press conference by the Committee in charge of the UN Year of the Elderly is still on. 'No idea,' he says cheerfully. LDC status reduces Madagascar's financial contribution to the UN, but also Madagascar's influence on, and interest in, the future direction of the rest of the world. My colleague spends his days drinking coffee in the UN canteen, until the UN's working day ends at around five o'clock. Then he meticulously collects all the literature produced by the bureaucracy that day and feeds it unread through a fax machine. Thus he sends roughly half a kilo of UN news per day to the foreign desk back home. Minutes of meetings, reports about hunger, resolutions pertaining to international peace and security, agreements concerning the worldwide eradication of polio. Rarely a word about Madagascar, and virtually nothing gets into the paper at home.

The UN Year of the Elderly Committee has so far managed to raise $5,000 in cash from the Member States. The year, dedicated to those over sixty-five, has 364 days left to run.

'Five thousand dollars, that's hardly a fortune,' I say, with concern.

'Depends on how you look at it,' replies my colleague. 'For Madagascar it would be more than enough. Our life expectancy is fifty-five.'

But first, there's a press conference on the world economic crisis, which is just about to begin. I ask if he's interested in coming. He thanks me, but declines: this crisis won't interest his readers either. Madagascar is too poor to suffer from it.

'The rainy season in the Sudan is almost over, which we regret.' The monotonous voice of UN spokesman Fred Eckhard recites the most recent list of resolutions designed to prevent international war and disaster. He sits at his table like a newsreader, with a little pile of papers in front of him. Squelchy Sudanese swamps will soon be drying out, bringing the prospect of further troop movements. 'We are therefore urging the Sudanese government to make haste in agreeing a cease-fire.'

After next dealing with the latest refugee crisis in Africa, he hands us over to today's guest speaker, an African from the UN Disarmament Commission. He is here to talk about the arms industry in relation to the world economic crisis and is just settling into his stride – 'In spite of all the hunger in the world, the arms race goes on . . .' – when Eckhard's voice resumes.

'I am sorry to have to interrupt,' he interrupts, 'but I am just hearing that the Security Council is going into session.'

The handful of journalists in the pressroom shake themselves awake, snatch their cassette recorders from under the African's chin and rush out of the door towards the escalator.

'I'll make photocopies!' the African calls after us. 'So you can read it through at home when you have a moment!'

By the time I have found the closed door of the Security Council, the session is well underway.

'Top secret,' says the guard and he visibly broadens.

'When are they coming out?' I ask.

'Dunno.'

For a moment I stand there nonplussed. Then I hear the clink of ice cubes and smell the fine vapour of Scotch and expensive cigars. Beyond the guard, and a little way to his left, there is a bar packed with diplomats. Locked out, just like me. Even the kings and presidents of countries being discussed are generally not allowed in. The minutes remain secret. Only the fifteen members of the Security Council know the details of the negotiations which lead to resolutions. They are the five permanent members (the USA, the UK, France, Russia and China) and the ten non-permanent members (who are allowed to sit in for two years after their election by the General Assembly). The privileged status of the Security Council has been a source of irritation since 1945, especially to those nations which, at any given moment, are not part of the 'Fabulous Fifteen'. This bar, right outside the Council door, is for diplomats representing the 176 excluded Member States. They call it their 'stake-out'. A beer costs $5 and a bourbon $10, but then the clientele is none of your usual riffraff.

'Sometimes they go through to midnight. Extremely humiliating to have to wait by the door for someone to take pity and throw you a crumb of information. To be treated just like you journalists,' says a senior Dutch official. For the past few months the Netherlands has been briefly reprieved from the nerve-wrecking ritual: she is enjoying her two-year stint as a non-permanent member. In evident satisfaction, he watches his colleagues from other Member States nervously clutching drinks as they wait for the end of the meeting. Their seats of government are waiting for news. 'We're finally sitting inside,' sighs the diplomat, thrilled.

'So you're allowed in,' snorts a Belgian representative. 'But that's all you're allowed. You can sit there if you like. Nothing more.' He speaks from experience. Belgium's stint as a non-permanent member preceded the Dutch: 'Resolutions were served up on a plate. Bill called Tony, Tony called Jacques, Jacques called Boris. By the time we were allowed to vote the case was completely sewn up.' Belgium, a Security Council member at the time, only heard that Operation Desert Fox was underway via CNN. America and Britain had gone into action while the Security Council was still meeting to discuss the next step in the Iraq crisis. A few hundred UN staff just had time to get to the Baghdad air-raid shelters before Anglo-American bombs began to rain down on their offices.

Easy chairs and coffee tables are scattered elegantly between tall houseplants. A blue crush barrier separates the bar from the Security Council door. The red plush corridor behind is thus preserved as a boulevard upon which the Fab Fifteen and their entourages can parade, as if on their way to a Hollywood première. We are the jealous public behind the barriers, staring.

Ladies come past, smiling amiably. 'Secretaries,' someone explains. An Armani suit emerges through the door and disappears to the Gents. 'Translator,' someone whispers. And then, suddenly excited, a colleague hisses: 'A Brit! He's going to leak something.' Before I know it, he has disappeared into a throng of diplomats and journalists pressing round the Englishman. I worm my way in and just catch his final words.

'. . . Russia is being difficult. That is all I can say.'

'Russia's always being difficult,' says one correspondent when the Brit is safely back inside. 'That's not news, is it? Or is it?' His colleagues are already on their mobile phones, so he takes out his own just in case.

'Lights!' shouts a media voice. Glaring TV lights snap on. The Asian who this month is chairing the Council appears in the doorway. A throng of microphones is thrust out in front of him as he announces that a new resolution has just been adopted. UNAMSIL, the UN peacekeeping force in Sierra Leone, is to be expanded from 13,000, to 17,000 men. 'The Security Council has instructed the Secretary-General to find the extra troops,' concludes the Chairman.

## II

*Sierra Leone, September 2000*

Something black and hairy shoots up the wall. 'Jesus! That was a rat!' cries Peter van Walsum, the Dutch representative on the Security Council. He stares at the air-conditioning vent into which the creature has wriggled, claws scraping. I fancy I catch him thinking: shall I scream and run away? Or stay cool and hope that it doesn't come back?

'Not such a little one either,' he says, allowing me a glimpse into his deliberations. 'What if I get bitten on the toe during the night?'

This is more than diplomatic whinging. Rats in Sierra Leone may carry the Lassa Fever virus, which can be deadly. OK, you can still find doctors, even here in war-zone Sierra

Leone. Indian blue helmets have transported a complete clinic from New Delhi to Freetown. 'But how do I get there in the middle of the night?' Van Walsum rhetorically demands. There is a curfew in force: anybody found on the street after 23.00 will be regarded as the enemy and 'removed'.

Van Walsum's sidekick, a young lady who has accompanied him from New York, offers to lodge a complaint with hotel reception. Maybe they can spray something or put something down. Van Walsum briefly considers this option, but then waves it away, 'Ach, let's just forget it.' If the world in general is imperfect, then Africa is especially so. Sometimes you have to live more in hope than in certainty.

Secretary-General Kofi Annan has failed to find the 4,000 extra troops for Sierra Leone. The Security Council has urged him, once again, to intensify his efforts. UNAMSIL is currently the largest peacekeeping mission on earth, in spite of which the rebels have begun to advance on the capital. 'Without reinforcements, this already faltering mission is in danger of being further undermined,' Mr Annan has told the world. Seventy-nine blue helmets have died since the start of the mission in 1999, and until very recently 500 UN personnel were being held hostage. Not a single Western country is militarily involved. The largest contributors to UNAMSIL are Nigeria, India and Bangladesh. Nor is it just here that the UN is struggling to find well-equipped and well-trained troops for its peace missions. Of the ten largest contributors to UN peacekeeping operations worldwide, nine are rated poor or below. India, Pakistan, Bangladesh, Jordan, Nigeria, Ghana, Kenya, Poland and the Philippines. Australia is a new entry to the top ten, having stepped into the breach in its own backyard, East Timor, in force.

'Has the West really done nothing since that resolution was adopted in May?' I ask Van Walsum.

'Well, not literally nothing,' he replies cautiously. 'The Dutch supplied a plane to take Jordanian blue helmets to Sierra Leone.'

Rumour has it that Canada has offered the same service to Bangladeshi blue helmets.

The UK has done something too. While refusing to provide any British troops for UNAMSIL, it has sent 300 paratroopers to train local government forces. 'Our self-respect is at stake here,' announced Foreign Secretary Robin Cook.

All the initiatives that Van Walsum has taken in the Security Council, designed to promote the involvement of industrialized countries in peace preservation in Africa, have been shelved or lost in the wastepaper basket. He has, for example, suggested to his own government that the Netherlands send a battalion of marines to Sierra Leone and encourage other European countries to do the same.

'I am naive,' says Van Walsum. 'OK, I had not really expected that battalion proposal to be accepted, but the ease with which it was swept from the table, without a single moment of serious consideration, almost as a reflex, that I found shocking, and not for the first time. It scared me. No white blue helmets in black Africa. That has become an unwritten law. But this just won't wash: approving UN missions in Africa, and then having nothing to do with them. Taking on the job, but letting others carry it out. I have found it extremely embarrassing to be representing my country in the Security Council when decisions on peace missions are being discussed.'

The diplomat is quite aware that Western absence from new peace operations derives from traumatic events in the recent past. America's refusal to take part in any UN mission proceeds from the UN 'debacle' in Somalia, where eighteen American soldiers lost their lives. Dutch non-participation stems from the drama in the Bosnian town of Srebrenica, where an estimated 7,000 Bosnian men were dragged off to their deaths by Serbian forces right under the noses of the Dutch UN contingent. And after the UN performance in Rwanda, almost the entire West has resolved to have nothing more to do with Africa.

'They don't want a repeat,' says Van Walsum. 'But what exactly are they trying to avoid?' Is it the slaughter of thousands of innocent people, or is it the shame of being implicated in another such drama.

'Give me one dollaaaaah!' screams an amputee on crutches. He pursues me, hobbling through the surf, as I stroll along the beach towards the bar. His left leg is missing below the knee, hacked off by a rebel chief who called himself General Blood-bath. The general also hacked off the right leg of this man's younger brother. He thought it was 'funny' to maim the two brothers symmetrically. The enemy against which the Security Council has dispatched blue helmets could be generously described as 'dangerously mad'.

I sit myself down next to an Indian UN officer. We're both drinking beer. CNN is on in the corner and Kofi Annan is talking about us. 'It is in Sierra Leone where the international community will have to show that the United Nations still has the right to exist, where it will have to be made clear that there really is something like solidarity between peoples that transcends race and geographical distance.'

'But of course there's something like solidarity between peoples,' cries the Indian indignantly. 'Western states are quite prepared to fight the rebels here down to the last Third World soldier.' He drains his glass and strides from the bar.

**A very serious question**

New York, 25 October 2001 — UN Secretary-General Kofi Annan said that Jordanian and Indian troops are being withdrawn from Sierra Leone because their governments had expected rich nations to join the UN force. The United Nations is still attempting to increase its force in Sierra Leone. Britain, the former colonial power, has announced that it will be raising its troop strength from 300 to more than 400 soldiers, but that it would not be part of the UN force. Jordan had hoped more troops would be provided by developed countries, said Mr Annan. 'They do not believe that the British offer is sufficient and had hoped that others would join.' But he conceded that they had at least 'made a gesture, while others have not.' Without mentioning the United States or others by name, the Secretary-General regretted the absence of troops from countries with large well-trained forces. 'This raises a very serious question that we all need to think through, not least the Security Council,' he said. 'Can the Council keep adopting resolutions that require us to deploy troops, while its own members do nothing, particularly those major countries with large forces?' he asked.                                    (Reuters)

Well, yes, the Council can.

'How did you arrive at that Sierra Leone resolution?' I had asked an American diplomat on the way out of UN HQ in Manhattan.

'You don't really want to know,' he replied. 'Resolutions are like hotdogs. If you know how they make 'em, you don't want to eat 'em. You just swallow. No questions asked.'

# 1. The UN in Somalia: Scuttled by Mutiny

## I

*Kenya, January 1994*

On the airport shuttle bus it's just like the school outing. The passengers, all blue helmets, have just flown from Mogadishu, Somalia, to the Kenyan resort of Mombasa, City of Sun and Fun. There is no lack of sun in Somalia, but that makes the lack of fun all the worse for the blue helmets stationed there. This lot are now on R&R, the UN's rest and recreation programme.

'Booz–ing! Fuck–ing!' chants a tall, skinny Irish soldier. He drags one of his comrades on to his lap and gropes exuberantly between his legs. Other blue helmets, all from Ireland, are lying all over each other clutching cans of Guinness.

'First time I've been out of that sandpit for five months. Nothing but whinging Somalis and the ugly mugs of my mates to look at. Mombasa, here I come!' cries one.

Three American soldiers, still teenagers, have opened a bottle of tax-free UN whiskey. 'Good food and hours in the bubble bath, ma'am,' is how they anticipate leave in Mombasa. And of course picking up girls at the Florida, the Mombasa disco which has assumed legendary proportions amongst blue helmets. The first groups of soldiers to return to Somalia after R&R could dazzle their colleagues with tales of leaving the Florida with three gorgeous babes on each arm. Currently your R&R counts as a failure if you haven't had at least six women tugging at your flies. I'd already picked up complaints in Nairobi. There were almost no whores left in the local bars. OK, a few ugly old ones, but all the pretty young girls were off to Mombasa.

'Beautiful and horny, that's what they say,' says one boy dreamily. His name, Willson, is stitched on his breast pocket.

'Eighty per cent have AIDS. Eighty per cent! You won't catch me taking a deep breath in the Florida tonight,' says one of the Irishmen.

'No sex at all. That is the only solution in Africa,' declares a German, still dressed in full kit.

'Bring any condoms?' I ask.

'Don't need 'em,' says Willson. 'I've decided. I don't fuck in Africa.'

'Me too. Same for all of us. But mates of mine who went into the Florida with the same good intentions still couldn't resist it. Drank too much to say No to the chicks. Now they can't sleep for worry. Because it's all left to the man. Those girls don't give a damn. With condoms, without, whatever you want, as long as you keep the Tia Maria and the cigarettes coming. They're all hooked on the Tia Maria.' This Irishman seems to know what he's talking about.

A Pakistani major in flowery shorts and flip-flops climbs in. He is the R&R officer for the UN Somalia operation and his job is to guide visitors through the UN's Mombasa amusement factory.

'Everybody retrieved their swimming trunks from the baggage carousel? Great! Then we'll be off to the hotel,' he cries happily. There are cowboy whoops and blue berets fly down the aisle.

Followed immediately by a deathly silence. The driver has left the parking area and the bus is nosing its way through the city's chaotic traffic: cars, ox carts, pedestrians. The sudden silence takes me by surprise and I turn and look back. The soldiers' fingers are dug into the backs of the seats in front of them. The knuckles are white.

'Happens every time,' whispers the Pakistani. 'The Somalia syndrome strikes again.'

I smile uncertainly.

'You can laugh,' says the Pakistani. 'But don't forget that there have already been more than sixty blue helmets killed in Somalia and there will be lots more to come. The Somalis are out to get us. The boys behind you feel like they've just walked straight into a nightmare. In Somalia they don't dare go out on the street any more. Unless for some urgent reason they have to leave the base, in which case they go in a tank. Here in Mombasa they are suddenly surrounded by Africans and they're not in a tank any more, just an old bus. What you see on their faces, madame, is pure terror.' My glance follows his nod and I see tightly shut eyes and heads sunk deep into shoulders, as if their owners were waiting for the blow to fall.

'No, lady, Somalia is no joke. The rats are leaving the sinking ship. All the Western countries are pulling their troops out. Those who have to stay are doomed.'

He stands up and cheerfully yells: 'Barbecue tonight, guys. And from twenty-two hundred hours, a free shuttle bus runs every half hour from the hotel to the Florida!'

He launches into 'We are the champions'. Nobody sings along except the Kenyan bus driver.


## II

Just suppose. Enough is enough. Narco-state Holland must be brought back into line with international drugs policy. The Dutch regime won't listen to UN resolutions, so now they must suffer the consequences: the UN sends blue helmets to close down the coffee shops. Any Dutch who resist can be shot. (And to complete this grisly projection, let's suppose that most of these blue helmets come from Third World countries, as is usually the case in reality. The daily rates paid by the UN – a nice extra in Western eyes – represent a fortune to the governments of poor countries. Ask an ex-Yugoslavian whom he saw wearing blue helmets during his country's civil war: in Bosnia there was even a contingent of Samburu warriors, straight from the deserts of northern Kenya. Tiny Bushmen from Botswana turned out for the UN in Somalia. In Rwanda it was largely Ethiopians and in Haiti, Djiboutis and Guatemalans.)

In the light of such a disturbing scenario, we can quite understand why the Member States have ensured that the UN Charter does not allow the UN to function as an independent organization – if the UN could take its own decisions, you might easily find yourself occupied by foreign troops.

The sovereignty of Member States is enshrined in the UN Charter. The Preamble begins: 'We, the peoples of the United Nations, determined [ . . . ] to reaffirm faith in the equal rights of nations large and small . . .' Chapter 2, Article 1 states: 'The Organization is based on the principle of the sovereign equality of all nations.' In the UN, therefore, all nations are equal and sovereign. All states, drug-crazed and decent, are free within their borders to do and allow what they want. They have nothing to fear from the UN, because from the sovereignty principle proceeds a non-intervention principle. 'Nothing contained in the present Charter shall authorize the United Nations to intervene in matters which are essentially within the domestic jurisdiction of any state . . .' (Chapter 2, Article 7). So if we see blue helmets somewhere in the world it is not because they have violently forced their way in, but because the government of the sovereign host country permits them to be there. This permission is valid for as long as the blue helmets behave themselves.

A close reading of the United Nations Charter allows only one conclusion: the UN can do nothing by itself. You could compare it to a computer, which only spews out what the user puts into it. Likewise the UN. It can only do what its Member States allow it to do.

Of the 191 Member States there are in fact five who determine whether or not blue helmets are despatched. These are the five permanent members of the Security Council: those old World War Two allies, the USA, France, Russia and the UK, later joined by China. Their task is 'to maintain international peace and security', although, in practice, the sovereignty and non-intervention principles mean that the task cannot be fulfilled. The UN cannot impose anything on Member States, peace or otherwise. All the Security Council can do is exert pressure, for example by calling upon Member States to boycott an undesirable regime until it steps down or stops misbehaving.

The USA, France, Russia, China and the UK have the right of veto over decisions made in the Security Council. This gives them, and only them, the power to scupper a peace mission, since every decision to send blue helmets must have the vote (or the abstention) of each of these five countries.

If the support of another four of the ten non-permanent members of the Security Council (each chosen for a period of two years) can be secured – giving a total of nine votes in favour – a mission can be despatched. In fact very few temporary members can afford to vote against a pet mission hatched by one of the Big Five. The superpowers have a whole arsenal of means at their disposal to secure the number of votes required.

### How America ran off with the Security Council

Twelve members of the Security Council voted for the resolution. One abstained. Two voted against. One of these, Yemen, had a particularly heavy price to pay. According to the *New York Times*, an American diplomat apparently snapped at the Yemeni representative that this would be the most expensive vote that Yemen had ever registered. 'Before the vote an American official visited our President. He handed him the American proposal for the resolution and said that America would be very grateful if Yemen were to support it.'

After Yemen had voted against it, the US scrapped the American aid budget for Yemen to the tune of $60 million. Colombia voted for the resolution. 'Our Achilles heel is drugs. America thinks that we don't act firmly enough against couriers. If we had voted against this resolution, or if we had abstained, then a sensitive boundary would have been crossed. We were very worried that the US would then repeat what they did to us two years before. On that occasion a Colombian judge had accidentally acquitted a drugs courier. This was the signal for retaliation. From that moment the American customs checked Colombian flowers box by box. The process took three to four days, by which time the flowers had wilted.'

(*Vrij Nederland*, 6 April 1991)

The five permanent members of the Security Council not only decide whether peace missions are sent or not. They also determine what the goal of these missions should be, what they can cost, how long they can last, how many blue helmets are needed and what powers they require to achieve their objectives. The UN computer churns out resolutions which summarize all these conditions, then prints the mandates in which blue helmets – sometimes – can read clearly where they should be and what they can and can't do. The mandates must be approved by the host country. Thus orders to blue helmets always sound something like: 'Do not fire except in self-defence and never on host country authorities.'

Not even when those authorities start slaughtering thousands of people under blue helmet noses?

Not even then.

In several missions blue helmets have been painfully confronted with this, the extreme consequence of the sovereignty and non-intervention principles: in Srebrenica (Bosnia) Serbian troops dragged several thousand Moslem refugees off to their deaths right in front of DutchBat (the Dutch UN battalion), while in Kibeho (Rwanda) it was ZamBat (from Zambia) who were forced to look on as more than 4,000 people died at the hands of Rwandan government forces.

Other, less extreme, consequences of UN principles also crop up from time to time: blue helmets handcuffed to lamp-posts (former Yugoslavia, summer 1995), blue helmets fleeing for their lives (from Rwanda, spring 1994). Such episodes clearly demonstrate how UN peace missions can turn into empty shows. They reveal, not blundering blue helmets, but what can happen when Member States, out of self-interest, choose a strict application of the sovereignty principle.

Even if this means that thousands of people might be massacred?

Yes. Even then.

★

The bloodier the consequences of the UN principles, the greater the pressure to wriggle out of responsibility. By consistently talking about the UN as if it were an independently functioning organization, the interested parties have succeeded in making the public believe that the UN has a life of its own. The suggestive language that governments use to make us believe that an independent UN really exists is actually a form of jargon, familiar but meaningless. Who has not heard the convenient slogans 'the UN should have intervened earlier', or 'more quickly', 'more efficiently', or 'with greater force'? Who has not agreed with the view that 'the UN must clean up its act' and 'reform', if these peace missions are ever to amount to anything? And are we not being constantly reminded that 'the international community' is avoiding its responsibilities and allowing whole peoples to perish?

If what is being implied here were true – namely, that 'the UN' (or the as yet undefined 'international community') can decide to intervene in the world – then it would follow that the UN (or the 'international community') could have chosen to close down, say, Dutch coffee shops long ago, but has decided not (yet) to do so. But you never hear the suggestion that the UN is too late, too slow, too inefficient or too weak to clean up Amsterdam. The misleading inference behind such a suggestion would immediately catch our attention. We only insist that 'the UN is failing' in devastated places like Somalia, Rwanda, Bosnia and Haiti, which in no way remind us of our fellow sovereign states. What we see there is chaos, misery and failing regimes. It is quite inconceivable that the same UN rules should apply both to them and to us.

We want 'somebody to do something' for these humanitarian disaster zones. What we would like best of all is for the wonderful world implied by the jargon to really exist, a world in which firm but fair blue helmets turn out to eliminate evil.

We want it so much that we succumb to the illusion. And governments encourage us to do so. Journalists and aid workers follow suit until finally we all end up believing in a world of our own invention, in which blue helmets are not doing what they could have been doing (had they been quicker, braver, more efficient, etc.). 'They are failing,' we say, with conviction.

'Governments lie. It is in their nature to do so,' writes the American journalist Mort Rosenblum in his book *Who Stole the News?* (1993). 'If governments are not deceiving their citizens with a preconceived goal in mind, then they are busy deceiving themselves. Deceiving yourself is an inborn human talent, and leaders are no exception. So leaders can lose sight of reality too.'

A good example of how deliberate deceit and wilful credulity can converge is provided by Médécins sans Frontières (MsF) and Oxfam. Since the news media report a steady stream of aid agency pronouncements on blue helmets and the UN, these organizations have a significant influence on public perceptions. In April 1995, MsF (also speaking for Oxfam) was denouncing the blue helmets present when more than 4,000 Hutus were killed in the Rwandan refugee camp at Kibeho. 'They stood by and did nothing,' thundered the MsF spokesman. 'They have blood on their hands.'

Reacting to these accusations, a foreign editor at the Dutch daily *de Volkskrant* wrestled bravely with the reality being ignored by the doctors: 'MsF is furious that UN soldiers stood by and did nothing in Kibeho. The UN always defends itself against moral indignation with the same argument: that the mandate for peacekeeping forces does not allow military action. This argument is valid enough but pales when set against shocking images of UN soldiers unable to do anything but drag away bodies' (28 April 1995).

The argument has in fact become so pale that it cannot stand up against even the most blatant demagoguery. President Clinton has made loaded language about the UN into an art-form. In his very first speech to the General Assembly (October 1993), the President announced that he was tired of the UN taking on tasks that were beyond its capacities. He was referring particularly to the UN peace mission in Somalia – already being portrayed as a 'UN fiasco' – with which America no longer wished to collaborate.

'The UN should learn to say No,' was Clinton's advice.

This was patent nonsense – the UN cannot say No if the Member States say Yes – but Clinton got away with it. Nobody raised any objection and journalists reported it without comment or reservation. In fact, the suggestion that the UN should learn to say No made the headlines worldwide.

Days later, on the inside pages, the UN argument made its pale reappearance through the mouth of Boutros Boutros-Ghali, the then UN Secretary-General. He would explain it yet again: 'It is not the UN which says Yes or No to anything. It is the Member States. The Member States said Yes to the mission in Somalia. The task of the Organization is merely to scrape together the troops and money required.'

By now reality has been swept so far under the carpet that it can be freely ignored when discussing UN peace missions. Talk about blue helmets as potential Globocops and nobody challenges you. Take blue helmets who obediently abide by the UN non-intervention principle, even when old ladies and children are being slaughtered in front of them, and you are free to accuse them of failure. No plaudits for military discipline in the execution of *our* mandate. Just outrage, scorn and contempt.

New York, 18 October 1993 – In Mogadishu
Boutros-Ghali was greeted by a hail of stones, and
in Sarajevo crowds spat at him and called him
'murderer'.                                    (*Newsweek*)

## Shamed

Thousands died in Srebrenica; Dutch soldiers wel-
comed the killers. A woman from Srebrenica said:
'DutchBat had the duty to defend us. Instead,
the Dutch Commander drank brandy with Mladic
himself . . .' After Srebrenica the nation that saw
itself as the protector of Anne Frank is being confronted with the possibility that its sons and daughters were accomplices to one of the most heinous
war crimes committed in Europe since the Second
World War.      (*Independent*, 21 September 1995)

## Blue helmets leave Rwanda

Kigali, 9 March 1996 – A frustrating mission that
failed to prevent genocide or protect refugees has
ended today. The UN flag was lowered by Indian,
Ghanaian and Malawian peacekeepers in Rwanda
to shouts of: 'Go home and don't come back!' A
Gurkha regimental band kept playing while
Rwandans jeered.                                (AP)

Clinton's 'the UN should learn to say No' was the signal
for Member States to start taking disciplinary action against
the UN. Ever since, politicians have increasingly linked the
'failure of the UN' to 'the inefficiency of the Organization' and to 'waste of money at UN Headquarters'. We
hear cries that 'the UN has become a bloated bureaucratic
monster' and that 'the UN is a bottomless pit'. The prospects

of the UN and its peace missions ever succeeding are therefore linked to 'economies', which in turn must lead to 'reforms'.

Member State USA leads the punitive chorus: the US, responsible for a third of the UN's annual budget during the 1990s, paid little or nothing for years until it owed the Organization the staggering sum of $1.3 billion. 'The American Senate will only move towards payment of its arrears in contributions when the UN takes concrete measures to lower costs and introduce reforms,' said Jesse Helms, Chairman of the Senate Foreign Affairs Committee (24 January 1997).

Other Member States have sensed their chance and enthusiastically cut back on their contributions, sometimes paying nothing at all. Governments can get away with it at home by suggesting that 'economies' are for the UN's own good, because they will lead to 'reforms'. They can get away with it in the UN because the Organization imposes no sanctions. Although the UN Charter does include penalties for defaulters (Member States can be stripped of their right to vote in the General Assembly), it is the Member States themselves who decide whether a sanction will be applied. Or not.

### Congress votes for limiting role in UN

Washington, 17 February 1995 – The House of Representatives has passed a bill designed to drastically limit the role of the United States in UN missions. The passage of the bill has been followed with increasing concern at UN Head Office in New York. Californian Congressman Rohrbacher summed up the views of the majority: 'After carrying the burden of world peace for forty years, it is time for America to give priority to her own interests. America comes first.' The debate on the new law was a long litany of complaint against the UN.

After the vote there were cheers and applause. 'This is a first step to ensure that in the future not a single American soldier will be forced to wear a blue beret and risk his life in countries where no American interests are involved,' said Republican Congressman Seastrand. The new law states that in principle American troops can no longer be deployed under UN command, arguing that US armed forces are too well trained and equipped to serve under non-American command. It is also proposed to reduce the US contribution from 31.7 to 25 per cent of the UN budget. Further, the cost of American actions such as those in Somalia and Haiti should be deducted from American contributions to blue helmet missions.

Republican presidential candidate Bob Dole also regards the UN as a discredited, badly led, superfluous, wasteful and, for American soldiers, dangerous organization.    (*de Volkskrant*)

### UN in financial difficulties

New York, 1 March 1995 – Two months after the final deadline for their 1995 contributions to the UN, only 19 of the 185 Member States have fully paid up. These are: Australia, Canada, Denmark, Finland, Iceland, Ireland, Kuwait, Liechtenstein, Luxembourg, Malaysia, Micronesia, the Netherlands, New Zealand, Norway, Pakistan, Singapore, Slovenia, Sri Lanka and Sweden.    (Reuters)

Sweeping 'economies', largely in the form of not very creative waves of redundancies, are therefore imposed on the Organization. But 'reforms' are conveniently forgotten. There is certainly no attempt to create anything that even slightly resembles an independently functioning UN that could nibble away at the sovereignty and non-intervention principles.

The apparatus charged with maintaining international peace and security is now expected to run on a budget equivalent to the amount that Americans spend at the florist each year. Peanuts, per capita. At the same time the UN directly employs fewer people worldwide than the advertising agency Saatchi and Saatchi.

The under-manning and poor equipment which afflict UN peace missions and which are direct consequences of withheld contributions, now contribute significantly to their failure.

### Peace missions: pursued on a wing and a prayer

New York, 29 December 1993 – In the UN's Department of Peacekeeping Operations, the daily 10 a.m. staff meeting is known as 'Morning Prayers'. As the peacekeepers gather each day to share the bad news on an alphabet of crises from Angola to the former Yugoslavia, they increasingly find themselves with little to offer beyond hopeful words. The meeting starts with a discussion of the situation in Angola. Warring factions have begun to negotiate a cease-fire. For the department's chief military advisor, a Canadian general, the prospect of a peace agreement means a potential problem. 'They'll say they want 25,000 peacekeepers in 30 days,' he said. 'We'll roll on the ground and start laughing.' Angola will line up with 17 other UN peacekeeping operations. The mission on the Kuwait–Iraq border has been waiting six months for 4,000 more soldiers; Bosnia has waited for 8,000 more since last May. If the troops also need equipment – a flak jacket, even a blue helmet – the average time to procure it is four months. To shorten delays, the Peacekeeping Department proposed setting up a stock of basic gear. But Member States refused to pay the $15 million needed to fund it.

One troop-contributing country has sent an unexpected message that its force in Rwanda will be pulling out sooner than expected. The department's biggest headache of the morning has been provided by the Americans. The US Army has just informed them that it will take all its equipment when the troops leave Somalia. Until now the US has said it would lease the UN its trucks, water purifiers and other gear essential to keep the mission running. 'They say, "You have our support", and then they do this,' said the General. Now he will have to scrounge the hard-to-find equipment from other nations.

It is time for the daily satellite phone call to Mogadishu. By Somalia's skewed standards, it has been a quiet day: a UN worker kidnapped, a bomb found in the UN compound, a fishing boat raided by pirates. 'The bomb – anything to do with the salaries of the police?' [The UN is training a new police force in Somalia and is responsible for paying their salaries – *author's note*.] When their pay is late, some law enforcers turn outlaw in protest. The Department promises to find the money.

(*Washington Post*)

The freedom that Member States permit themselves in deciding whether or not to contribute to the upkeep of the UN is also extended to decisions crucial to the success of UN peace missions. Member States are free to send troops to peace missions or not. And they are free to share the cost of peace missions or not. And Member States cynically abuse this freedom. The cost of achieving the objectives set for peace missions is rapidly deemed too high. National interests always prevail above (international) UN goals.

In Somalia men and equipment assigned to the UN were often withdrawn prematurely, leaving blue helmets from other Member States empty-handed in a war zone. Financial contributions pledged to the mission by other Member States were simply not paid, sometimes with fatal consequences. Some governments also instructed their blue helmets to ignore UN orders that would place them at risk. Thus the UN's Operation Continue Hope in Somalia was scuttled by the mutiny of its own Member States.

The Americans, who initiated and commanded the mission, first holed the ship and then abandoned it, accusing those who were left on board. Of failing. Of not being able to say No.

### Americans pull out of Somalia

Washington, 15 October 1993 – After the death of 18 American soldiers in Mogadishu, President Clinton has decided to end US military operations in Somalia. When American troops have left, the US will make no further funds available for the UN in Somalia.

The UN is warning that the whole future of the operation is now at risk, since other countries could follow the American lead and withdraw. (Reuters)

The American lead was indeed followed, as with the payment (or non-payment) of contributions:

### Italy and Egypt want to quit Somalia

New York, 16 October 1993 – Italy is to withdraw its 2,600-man force from Somalia. According to the Italian Minister of Defence, the announcement of the American withdrawal has played a role in this decision. UN officials hope that African and Asian troops will fill the gaps. Pakistan already has 5,000 men in Somalia and India 3,600. One problem, however, caused by the UN's financial crisis, is that the UN is behind with payments for participation in its peacekeeping missions. Many countries are therefore no longer willing to provide troops. Egypt, which has more than 500 men in Somalia, is among countries to have announced that they will withdraw if arrears are not quickly paid.                                   (AFP)

### Turkish army wants to get out of Somalia

Ankara, 17 October 1993 – The Turkish high command has advised the government in Ankara to pull the 320 men they have stationed in Somalia out before the end of their term, now that it is becoming increasingly clear that the operation is crumbling away.                              (AP)

### Greece withdraws troops

Athens, 19 January 1994 – Greece will this week begin withdrawing its military forces from Somalia. Defence Minister Gerasimos Arsenis did not give a reason. Of the 100 Greek soldiers currently in Somalia, 70 will return home before the end of this week.                                        (AP)

## III

*Somalia, February 1994*

'What about tomorrow morning, seven o'clock, UN flight 283? Or is that a bit on the early side for you?'

It looks like the business check-in of a regular airline. The hostess, in a baggy camouflage uniform, zealously consults the schedules on her computer screen. She looks up apologetically: 'Oh, what a pity! The next flight is not until quarter past twelve and that makes a stopover too. So shall we make it the early flight, then?'

I hurriedly nod in agreement. Less than ten minutes ago I'd been certain that getting a lift with the UN into Somalia would mean pulling out all the stops.

'Window or aisle?' she asks me next morning. A blue UN label is attached to my backpack, which then disappears on to a baggage trolley.

The transport aircraft is like a hangar inside. Rows of old cinema seats are screwed to the floor. The cockpit is separated from the passenger area by a sheet of flapping canvas. Stacked cool boxes labelled 'Human Blood' are lashed down with chains just behind me and a spare tyre trembles on a hook very close to my head. It is stifling: without air-conditioning the temperature rises to tropical heights. The soldier next to me produces a diplomatic briefcase. He fishes out a report as thick as a fist and snaps it open with a sigh. Not an easy read, to judge by his expression. On the other side of the gangway a blue helmet dozes off behind a copy of the *Kenya Times*.

The flight lasts only a couple of hours. The country below us grows ever more barren and then comes the desert. Mogadishu-on-Sea is hemmed in by yellow sand dunes. As it approaches the runway, the plane skims so low over the waves that I can see great fish swimming in the clear water.

The passengers jerk awake as the stewardess, shrouded in camouflage, signs off over the intercom: 'On behalf of the captain and his crew, I would like to wish you a pleasant stay in Mogadishu!'

My fellow travellers don their blue helmets and snap magazines into their machine guns. The stewardesses draw their pistols before opening the doors. I am the last to descend the steps to the asphalt.

'Madame! What are you doing here, for God's sake?' I am being addressed in Flemish. It is an officer awkwardly clamping a six-pack of Fanta under his arm. His surprise is nothing compared to my amazement at the bewildering activity raging on the tarmac. Hot dust, thrown up by turbulence, swirls in my face. White helicopters are landing and taking off all around me. Beyond them, a little Fokker noisily leaves the ground, which is trembling beneath tanks roaring off to the perimeter and disappearing between green army tents. Trucks and jeeps rip along the sandy verges of the runway.

The aircraft steps which I have just descended are now being climbed by a battalion of Pakistanis, all in white pyjama trousers topped by black singlets and all sporting the same black moustache. They are followed by a bunch of Indian Sikhs wearing UN blue turbans in place of blue helmets.

Of the other troops marching past I can only make out the top lips: blue helmets are pulled down deep over eyes and bullet-proof vests stretch up over chins. Nobody is unarmed. Soldiers with mortars look down from the roofs of the hangars. Machine guns are dangling from the necks of the men emptying the aircraft hold. Other soldiers pass with drawn pistols. I am standing slap-bang in the middle of Continue Hope, the United Nations' peacekeeping mission to Somalia.

'Hey! Are you trying to get yourself killed or what?' The Belgian is still staring at me in astonishment.

'I . . . er . . . am looking for . . . um . . . a taxi into town,' I manage to stammer.

'A taxi? There are no taxis here. No town either, not any more,' says the Belgian.

But there's no time to take the matter further. We have to clear the runway for the arrival of another thundering transport plane. The Belgian tugs me by the sleeve into a white hangar where soldiers are clutching their weekend bags and waiting: the departure hall. A young man in civvies, notebook in hand, is interviewing a nun.

'You a reporter?' the Belgian demands. 'This lady's a colleague of yours, I believe.' And without further ceremony he runs off to a waiting white helicopter and is lifted away.

'So it's your first time in Mogadishu,' states the young man, uninvited. 'I'll give you a ride to the Al Sahafi. That's where the press stays. I'm John.'

Discarded plastic bottles, escaped from the UN bases, blow through the streets in their thousands. A permanent dust- and sandstorm rages unimpeded through the town. Mogadishu has become transparent. Only the carcass remains. Bits of roof litter the roads and dunes of drifting sand advance from the surrounding desert through the shattered walls of flats and shopping arcades towards the city centre. The rubble is closely guarded: young Somali warriors parade on top of it, their robes flapping around their long, thin legs. The machine guns slung over their shoulders on ropes look much more impressive than the boys themselves. Most are barely sixteen and skinny as rakes.

Al Sahafi is Arabic for 'The Journalists'. And journalists, usually no more than four or five at a time, are the only guests that Ali, the hotel's owner, still gets. The Al Sahafi is the only hotel still functioning in Somalia. When the civil war reached the capital and it had become too dangerous for press agency correspondents to stay in their offices, Ali had opened his steel gates. The four-storey building stands in the centre of town, exactly halfway between the two UN bases – Port, on the ocean, which covers the harbour and the airport, and Embassy, on the other side of town, where blue helmets are camping on the debris of the former US Embassy. From the flat roof of the hotel I can just make them out: both are shrouded in thick clouds of dust.

Some way off shore, two American warships are riding gently at anchor, waiting to take off the last few American soldiers. The light is now turning from orange to red and the setting sun seems to fill half the horizon. A white UN helicopter passes across it. A flock of white ibises, in V-formation, flaps by in the wake of the colossal machine.

'Makes the chopper look like Mother Goose,' says John, giving his satellite phone a clean. He flicks grains of sand away with his handkerchief. There are no ordinary telephone links between Mogadishu and the outside world any more. Telegraph poles lie snapped across the roads. The poles that still stand no longer carry any wire. Each hotel guest has installed his own transmitter on the roof.

'And look, there's the 6.30 Hercules.' The great plane comes ponderously in over the sea. 'I hope they've got a few crates of printer ribbon on board. You can't get 'em here any more and I've nearly run out.'

The Al Sahafi stands next to a concrete triumphal arch, now riddled with bullet holes. It is a copy of the entrance gate to the Colosseum in Rome. An aid agency has pasted posters of screwdrivers, pliers and machine guns to the pillars. The pictures are torn and faded. After the tools you can still just read 'Yes!', and after the guns 'No!'. When the peace mission began, the UN invited weapon owners to begin a new life and offered to turn them from snipers into builders. Since then there has been less and less work for builders. More and more for snipers.

Piles of burned-out cars surround the triumphal arch. They have been stripped to the bodywork. Trucks, cars with no wings or bonnets, camels and sputtering Vespas worm their way between hundreds of hand carts. The city can't get enough wheelchairs. I see so many cripples with stumps instead of legs stumbling past, I lose count. Some have converted wheelbarrows and are being pushed round the holes in the road by loved ones. Others, sitting on planks with wheels, are being pulled through them by donkeys.

Shattered minarets and bombed-out apartment blocks protrude above the treetops. Almost all the houses have been abandoned by their original inhabitants and refugees have moved in to sleep on the rubble. Opposite the Al Sahafi Hotel, on the roof of what used to be the Egyptian Embassy, a group of blue helmets is camped. Their sandbags are piled high from the gutters. The largest bullet holes in the façade have been crudely filled with cement and all the windows are boarded up. I focus my binoculars. The soldiers have hung out their washing on cables and antennae. One of them is stirring a large pan of soup – it is nearly dinnertime. When a muezzin issues the call to evening prayer from the tower of a blackened mosque, the blue helmets fall devoutly to their knees.

'Pakistanis,' explains John.

I pivot round to another roof full of blue helmets. One of them has binoculars too. He catches me in his sights and waves. I wave back.

'Making friends?' asks John. 'I'd watch out with people like that. Peacekeepers are the enemy here. I always make a detour if I come across a UN patrol in town. The clans like to take pot shots at them.'

He is still talking when there is the sound of gunfire. Before I know it, John is lying flat on his belly. Further up the street, a line of people waiting by the well scatters. A man falls and stays down. Dead, I think.

When the shooting stops, the line reforms as if nothing has happened. The dead man is quietly stepped over.

John grins uneasily as he stands up. 'The day before yesterday a mortar went off right under my window. My hair is still full of chalk from the ceiling.' He bangs some dust out of his sleeves. 'I've got a joint left. Want to share it? Calms you down. Me anyway. I'm terrified here, you might as well know it. Thank God the Americans are gone in two weeks, 'cos that will be it for me too. For all of us, actually. The readers aren't interested in the Third World troops that are staying behind.'

He is not even a real journalist, he admits, exhaling a fragrant cloud of smoke. He was an American student backpacking through Africa when he met a press agency editor in a Kenyan bar who offered him a job in Somalia. Flattered, John set off for Mogadishu at once, quite unaware of the fact that press agencies can't get their own people to follow this war. Nobody wants to do it. The Somalis shoot at journalists too.

The sun has disappeared and the city has gone pitch-dark:

leaving a generator running means valuable diesel. Anyway, sooner or later anyone who owns such a machine has it stolen by roving gangs. I count precisely eight houses with lights in this city of a million inhabitants.

Down in the street one of these precious generators starts up and a movie screen appears. The cinema has lost its roof and the top half of its walls. From our high position we enjoy the top half of the main feature, a tired Hollywood version of the hell that was Vietnam. GIs, with faces smeared green, hack a path through the jungle and raze Vietcong territory flat. 'A day without blood is a day without sunshine,' groans a wounded American sergeant, who is being extracted from a Vietcong spear.

'Hear that? Great lesson for those Pakistanis across the street,' says John.

'You bet,' I say.

Straight after dinner (spaghetti, served up in a windowless back room) there is a thud which shakes the walls of the hotel. A mortar shell has hit our Pakistani neighbours, reports the owner. I run up to the roof and find John with his ear pressed to a scanner.

'You still alive? Over!' says an American voice from one of the UN camps.

'Yes, sir, but big hole in our wall, sir. Over!' crackles the reply. The roll of the Ls puts me right back in Pakistan.

'So where the hell are you? Over!' barks the American.

'If you turn left by the Al Sahafi, sir . . .' the Pakistani begins helpfully.

'Nobody knows where the hell that place is, man. Just give me the co-ordinates!'

'They don't know that this place exists up at the UN bases,' says John. 'They've even forgotten that Mogadishu still exists.

Most governments won't let their blue helmets out on the
street any more.'

In the distance the two UN camps shine brighter than stars.
Ferocious floodlights bathe the ground in a searing white light.
I can hear the dull drone of the UN generators. Ships and
aircraft are being loaded with US Army containers. In the
harbour giant cranes swing out jeeps on long chains. The bases
are bursting with light and life in the dark and silent city.

But down in the alleys, I catch the flickering blue light of
gas-fired welding torches. The more American weaponry is
shipped home, the more the Somalis dare to bring their own
heavy artillery back into play. They are now busy welding
machine guns to stands in the backs of their pickup trucks, so
they can shoot while driving.

Untroubled by cheaper competitors, Ali, the Al Sahafi's
owner, demands $85 a night. For this modest price the guest
is free to enjoy walls riddled with bullet holes and beds full of
sand which has blown in through them. Ali survives as a
businessman in Somalia because he pays protection money to
the most important clans. And he protects himself against
gangs operating independently of the warlords with weapons
drawn from his private arsenal in the cellar.

The bored Somali hustlers who hang around the high-
walled courtyard of the Al Sahafi are the same type you find
in hotels all over the world. But in Mogadishu it is not
wooden carvings or black market currency they are selling. It
is bodyguard services. If I want to leave the hotel I need a car
and two armed guards. I assume that the standard tariff of $100
a day includes protection money.

'Sure, protection for the car, not for you,' says John, punc-
turing my illusion.

From the array of candidates I choose the two with the

shiniest Kalashnikovs, in the use of which, they assure me, they are exceptionally skilled. As a driver I take the one whose car has a spare tyre in the boot. It has no windows, but that is par for the course.

The driver and the bodyguards are all called Mohammed and are stoned on khat. One of them already has a layer of down on his upper lip. At seventeen, he's the eldest of the three.

John has stuck his head through a door and is overwhelming me with survival tips. His thing is rapid interviews with clan chieftains in burned-out houses, or aid workers in half-ruined offices, after which he gets driven back to the hotel like a bat out of hell.

'Sometimes we get shot at, and my bodyguards shoot back. They haven't hit us so far. We haven't hit them either: my guys only stole their Kalashnikovs a year ago and they're not yet sure how they work,' he laughs sourly. 'But I always hire the same guys, because I don't dare to fire them. They'd take revenge.'

The head of Ali, the hotel owner, appears through the other door. He presents me with his collection of souvenirs. While he still has the chance.'

'Buy?' It is not really a question. I take a 'General Aideed, Lion of Africa' calendar and a very black T-shirt bearing the slogan 'Mogged Out', journalist shorthand for 'Murdered in Mogadishu'.

'Never come back the same way you went,' John rattles on. 'Bandits may be waiting to ambush you.'

One Mohammed climbs in behind the wheel and the other two clamp me tight between them on the back seat. The engine starts. John is still talking: 'Remember, mobs are more dangerous than mortars. And whatever happens, keep driving. Make sure your man keeps his foot down.'

'To the United Nations. Presto!' I command. The three Mohammeds speak better Italian than English, the legacy of their former colonial masters. They snap the clips into their weapons and the hotel gate slams shut behind us.

My blood runs cold: we are immediately stuck in a herd of camels.


## IV

In 1992 aid agencies were reporting that famine was threatening to kill half the Somali population 'at the rate of 3,000 a day'. Because of a civil war, food aid was no longer getting through to the hungry. Five hundred blue helmets from Pakistan could not deter the bandits who were threatening the food convoys. America decided to get involved.

> **America to invade Somalia**
> Washington, 27 November 1992 – President Bush is prepared to send an army of 20–30,000 men to Somalia to act as protection for humanitarian aid in the shattered East African country. 'We are deeply concerned about the fate of the Somali people,' said a White House spokesman. (Reuters)

The US Army's task was to ensure that food convoys could reach the hungry without being robbed on the way. The Americans christened the planned intervention 'Operation Restore Hope'. They also demanded, via a Security Council resolution, that Restore Hope would be followed by a UN peacekeeping mission, against which the main Somali clan leaders were said to have no objection. With famine avoided, the UN was to come in and establish peace, offering a new future to the ravaged country. 'Operation Continue Hope' was the name the Americans were already using for this second phase of the plan. The Security Council agreed.

Two days before the invasion was due to land in Somalia a messenger from President George Bush apparently arrived in Mogadishu. 'Look,' he said to the duly assembled Somali clan leaders, 'under American leadership the world is going to stop this country committing suicide. The President of the United States is quite determined. We come in peace, but you know what the American Army can do. You've seen it for yourselves during Desert Storm. Now those same American forces will be landing here the day after tomorrow. If you don't co-operate, we will pulverize you.'

The invasion was shown live on prime-time television. It was the easiest the world had ever seen. American soldiers landed on the beach at Mogadishu blinded by the flashlights and floodlights of the international media. There was not a Somali in sight. The US Army took over the port and the airport and the first food convoy, guarded by American soldiers, was soon on its way. CNN followed up with moving pictures of GIs, covered with recently fed Somali children singing 'Jingle Bells' at the tops of their voices. It was 9 December 1992, the run-up to Christmas.

In spite of their impressive entry – 20,000 fighting troops roaring up in their tanks, helicopters and hovercraft – the US high command was determined not to intervene in the power struggle being fought out between the Somali clans. That would be much too dangerous. Before you knew it, you'd land up in a guerrilla war. Besides, the future of Somalia, for which the clans would have to make peace with each other, was one of the tasks reserved for the UN mission that was soon to follow.

'If you leave us and the food convoys alone, we'll leave you alone,' was thus the American proposal to the clan leaders. Who could scarcely believe their luck. They could all keep their weapons, as long as they didn't point them at Americans. A request to disarm the clans, absolutely vital in the UN view (expressed by Boutros-Ghali) if peace was to have any chance, was flatly refused. Again, far too dangerous. When, a week after the invasion, an American officer saw his men confiscate a machine gun from a Somali, he promptly ordered them to return it.

### Somalia will not be disarmed

New York, 17 December 1992 – 'For a Somali three things are really important,' says an American spokesman in Somalia, 'his wife, his camel and his gun. The right to own a weapon lies deep in the Somali soul. If a foreigner threatens to use violence to disarm him, he will immediately cry "over my dead body". Forced disarmament would be regarded as blatant colonialism by the Somalis.'

(*de Volkskrant*)

'Besides,' said the Americans, 'disarming Somalia would be impossible. Everyone in this country has a gun, a grenade or a knife in his pocket. What hasn't worked in Los Angeles will be ten times harder in Mogadishu.'

The Somali civil war dragged on, but food convoys were no longer attacked since US soldiers were riding shotgun. Five months after the invasion the famine was over and America's 'Operation Restore Hope' duly became the United Nations' 'Operation Continue Hope'.

### Mission half accomplished

To the US military, the job is finished. The hand-off to the UN officially began on May 1 when Secretary-General Boutros-Ghali started paying the bills. US troops are streaming home. By June 1 only 4,000 will remain – 1,300 as a rapid-deployment unit, plus 2,700 others left in charge of logistics . . . President Clinton greeted soldiers just home from Somalia in a photogenic ceremony on the White House lawn. 'Your successful return reminds us that other missions lie ahead for our nation. You have proved that American leadership can help mobilize international action to create a better world,' he said.

(*Time Magazine*, 17 May 1993)

Blue helmets and UN negotiators took over US positions in Somalia, with military and logistical backup from the remaining American units.

The US also retained military command of the operation under the UN flag: an American general was named UN Force Commander in Somalia, with 28,000 blue helmets from thirty-three countries and 300 civilian personnel under his command. It was the largest UN operation to date.

The blue helmets had scarcely landed when they received orders from their American commander to begin searching for weapons. Those who refused to let the blue helmets disarm them had their houses shelled by the Americans. Hundreds of Somalis were killed.

The bloodier the American bombardment, the more violent the Somalis became in their anger at foreign soldiers in general: more than sixty blue helmets (from Pakistan, Italy, Egypt, Nigeria and Nepal) were killed by Somali bullets.

The UN peace mission was already fully embroiled in a war with the Somalis, with the self-proclaimed General Aideed leading the most bloodthirsty opposition, when the Americans suddenly announced that they would be pulling out all their remaining forces. The deaths of eighteen American soldiers in a single day were deemed to be too high a price for American support of the UN mission – a mission the US itself had initiated. The American public would never stand for it.

### Firefight from Hell

18 October 1993 – It started out as a working Sunday . . . Not long after breakfast Somali spies on the CIA payroll reported that three of Aideed's top lieutenants were holding a meeting that after-noon at the Olympic Hotel . . . Here was a chance to decapitate the Somali senior command. At about 1.30 p.m. the Rangers' commanding officer put the finishing touches to a plan to snatch the Somalis. To maintain secrecy, details were kept from UN forces, which are infiltrated with Aideed spies. A raiding party of about 60 Rangers and Delta commandos piled into about eight MH-60 Black Hawk helicopters. Some would land on the hotel's roof and grab the Somali leaders. Others would alight across the street and provide covering fire. A ground convoy of some 30 Rangers would truck everyone back to base . . . Suddenly, everything started to go terribly wrong. The Humvees ran into an ambush. Three Black Hawk helicopters were brought down . . . By 7.00 US commanders were desperately trying to assemble rescue forces. They hadn't anticipated the difficulties of a joint US–UN operation. Malaysian and Pakistani

officers had the only tanks and armoured personnel carriers available in all of Mogadishu for the mission. But foreign UN troops put up some resistance. They had been left out of the loop on the Ranger assault, and balked at revving up their armored vehicles. Newsweek has learned that at one point, a US officer held a gun to the head of a Pakistani tank commander to force him to move out with the rescue party. On their way to the Olympic Hotel, a rocket-propelled grenade struck an APC, killing the Malaysian driver and wounding his machine gunner.                    (*Newsweek*)

A CNN camera crew, who happened to be on the scene, filmed the body of one of the eighteen dead Americans being dragged through Mogadishu on a rope, as a trophy. American TV viewers, who had long forgotten where Somalia was, woke up with a start.

### TV pictures shock America

Washington, 6 October 1993 – Members of the American House of Representatives and of the Senate have called on President Clinton to immediately withdraw American troops from Somalia.

'Enough is enough,' said a Republican spokesman. 'We must ensure that we get out of there as quickly as possible.'                    (Reuters, AP)

Clinton promptly pronounced that the mission to Somalia was a UN failure: the UN should have said No to Somalia. Nobody pointed out that the whole operation, dreamed up by America, had been under American command from start to finish. Except, of course, Boutros-Ghali.

### Boutros-Ghali America's greatest critic

18 October 1993 – Boutros-Ghali has had to swallow his anger at the American withdrawal from Somalia. 'I must remain practical. I cannot allow myself a confrontation with such an important UN member. I need America.'

He had listened with astonishment to Clinton's speech to the UN, in which the American President reproached the UN for repeatedly shouldering tasks that were too heavy for it. 'The UN should learn to say No,' said Clinton.

'It is not the UN which says Yes or No to anything. It is the Member States. The Member States said Yes to the mission in Somalia. The task of the Organization is only to scratch together the troops and money required for missions,' says Boutros-Ghali. He has repeatedly described his task as 'going begging round the capitals of the world'. 'To be clear: I have no power and I am not independent. The Member States of the UN are free to help pay for peace missions or not. The Member States are free to make troops available or not. To be able to do my job, I am dependent on your goodwill.'                    (*International Herald Tribune*)

By the time I arrive, orders from Washington have prohibited any further US involvement in Continue Hope. American troops are to devote their few remaining weeks in Somalia exclusively to breaking up their camps in Mogadishu. The city is strewn with the burned-out and plundered wrecks of UN tanks and armoured vehicles. It is still war on the streets, as it was before the US invasion, only now the UN has become one of the parties. There is still no employment, no civil authority and no Somali government with whom the UN command can negotiate. All the UN can expect from a peace agreement with one clan is declarations of war from all the other clans. Without American backup, most blue helmets refuse to go out on the streets. If movement is necessary they usually now go by helicopter.

> New York, 10 January 1994 – Boutros-Ghali has proposed keeping a peace force of 16–20,000 soldiers in Somalia after the departure of US and other forces. He said that his proposal is based on what the United Nations can deliver, not on what they regard as necessary. Boutros-Ghali is doubtful whether the remaining soldiers will have sufficient support and financial means at their disposal to be able to accomplish anything. Lack of logistical support is particularly acute. In spite of urgent appeals, not a single UN Member State has agreed to send such personnel.          (Reuters, AFP)

## V

The occasional blue flag, bleached by the sun and frayed by the wind, flutters above the high walls. Around the forest of barbed wire that encircles the UN Base 'Embassy' prowl inhabitants of Mogadishu, young and old. Like jackals wearing down their prey, they keep the UN stronghold surrounded day and night, their hungry eyes searching for unguarded openings, greedily absorbing the sounds and smells that rise from the camp. Within the walls, reinforced with sandbags and broken glass, there is an abundance of everything that the destitute Somalis lack: fuel, food, water and protection from roving gangs.

Exclusive possession provokes deadly envy. Pakistani peace-keepers, armed to the teeth, stand guard by the only two entries that provide access to the cornucopia within. Most of them skulk in what look like wooden wildlife observation hides: when my bodyguards and I drive up, all that appears in the lookout slit are eyes, machine-gun barrels and a glimpse of blue helmet. Two Pakistanis creep reluctantly out of their hutch. They are a bit like the Keystone Kops, with the same generous moustaches and the same truncheons.

All attempts to disarm the Somalis have been stopped by the new (Turkish) UN Commander and blue helmets can only open fire if they are fired upon first. The Somalis infallibly sense the helplessness of the UN peacekeepers without American backup: the Pakistanis at their checkpoints are being plagued by hordes of self-confident, taunting youths and even by six-year-old children. Orders are to ignore empty Coke cans thrown at the head. Hitting is still allowed (if the screaming kids come too close) and the Pakistanis keep their UN batons at the ready. But the children are quick as lightning. Distracted by our arrival, one blue helmet lets his sunglasses be snatched from his nose. The other finds himself pulling his gun from the hands of a couple of beanpole adolescents. He looks like a dopey small-town cop.

'Give it back!' he shouts. And when he finally succeeds, he pulls a chain out of his trouser pocket and locks the weapon to his belt.

It is not easy for my Mohammeds to nose their way through the crowd of children. One of the Pakistanis squats down low behind the car door, using the car as a buffer between the seething mass and himself.

'Permit, please.' He studies my press card while throwing uneasy glances around him then gestures to us to follow him. Scything with his baton, he clears a path for us through to the UN gates.

The small sand compound behind the gates is full of parked tanks in a variety of sizes. The heads of more Pakistanis protrude from the turrets. The barrels point nervously towards the street.

I ask if it's always so heavy around the entrance. The Pakistani soldier nods indignantly. 'I had never thought I should come to hate children, but those kids out there are monsters,' he says. 'This morning one little devil appeared on top of our sandbags. "Saa, saa," I shouted and waved my stick to chase him away. He couldn't have been more than nine. He just stood there grinning. Then he suddenly produced a grenade out of his pocket, pulled out the pin and threw it down right in front of me. And all the time he kept grinning. Luckily the grenade didn't go off. Otherwise I'd be dead.'

We come to an inner wall, where Turkish soldiers man a narrow concrete passage known as the Turkish Gate. It is equipped with a metal detector. The final screening of visitors takes place here. My Mohammeds join the collection of body-guards who wait by their cars until their clients (aid agency people) reappear through the Turkish Gate. I tag on to the end of a line of recruits for Mogadishu's new police force. Their predecessors have removed themselves to a foreign country, along with the old President. It is the UN's job to replace them. Installing a political committee in every district and a police force in every village is to be the first step towards Somalia's future. The blue helmets just have to hope that it works: the budget won't stretch much beyond recruiting and equipping the country's new force. UN Member State Japan has provided a few million dollars for police training (as an alternative to sending peacekeepers) but the gift will not cover the costs. On their appointment, the twenty Somali cadets were issued with the top half of a uniform. They now jostle barefoot to be first through the detector: between theory lessons they get a free lunch served inside the base. Beyond the UN walls, food is unaffordable or available only from aid agencies.

Ali, the recently appointed Police Commissioner of Moga-dishu, is already through. He and some of his men are sitting under a Turkish canopy of corrugated iron, flicking flies away with their wraparound skirts.

'You'll never guess what the UN want now,' he grumbles. 'They want us to disarm the clans! We haven't a chance. My men and I are utterly powerless. The UN has given us ten machine guns to share between twenty. We are lucky the clans have left us alone so far. If they attack us, we'll just have to hope that our ammunition has arrived. Maybe they are waiting until we get our police cars. Then robbing us will be worth the effort.'

Before I can leave to search the base for the American press conference, Ali asks whether I might perhaps know when he and his men are next going to be paid. It is already a couple of months since the UN came up with the goods. Do they really want his brand new police force to go stealing?

The American spokesman is a dove-grey, freshly shaved appar-ition in a camouflage uniform with short tropical sleeves and knife-edge creases. He presents himself smiling behind a wooden lectern in the pre-fab office that houses the United States Information Service, USIS.

The map of the city which adorns the wall does not show any streets (but then, many streets in Mogadishu are no longer recognizable as such). Instead the town is divided into danger zones, outlined in red, with here and there a green cross to indicate the position of a Pakistani checkpoint.

'We are nicely on schedule,' begins the spokesman. 'Currently on the ground: 3,021 American military personnel. That is 453 fewer than yesterday. The evacuation of the US Army is proceeding according to plan. In two weeks we will all be gone. Any questions?' He looks cheerfully round the room.

Apart from me, the only journalists taking their seats on the folding wooden chairs this morning are a reporter from Radio UNOSOM (the news station for UN soldiers based in Somalia) and someone from the information magazine produced by the UN for the Somali population to read. Every week the new edition is distributed from high-flying military helicopters: too many house-to-house delivery personnel were murdered during their rounds of Somali letterboxes. Also present to hear today's good news is a DJ from Radio America, which is keeping American soldiers amused with Country Music and Rock 'n' Roll as they wait to be evacuated. I raise my finger.

'When is the new police force going to be paid again?' I ask on behalf of Ali. The spokesman keeps smiling.

'No idea,' he replies. 'That has nothing to do with the US Army. For the reconstruction of Somalia you must apply to the UN. Anyone else? Nobody? OK then, have a nice day everybody.'

The storm of sand and dust which rages even inside Base Embassy clogs the nose, eyes and lungs, while the racket from thousands of generators, large and small, almost drowns out the din of helicopters skimming low over the tents. The American Embassy in Mogadishu was the largest and most expensive that the US had ever established south of the Sahara.

It was equipped with swimming pools, tennis clubs and even a technical high school, at which the children of the local elite were most welcome. Less than a year after its official opening this diplomatic paradise had to be abandoned. The clans, in their struggle with government forces, had advanced to the gates of the city and American diplomats were hastily evacuated.

The militias began by plundering the deserted complex: toilet bowls, wash-hand basins, doors and tennis nets were carried out. Electric sockets were chipped out of the walls and removed. Then the warriors flattened the buildings. Piles of rubble from luxurious residences and sports clubs are now scattered over a sandy area the size of several football pitches. On top of it all stands a tent city built to accommodate 14,000 blue helmets, half the force involved in Continue Hope when still at full strength. The other half was based at Port, the military camp that had grown up around Mogadishu's airport and harbour. Nobody knows precisely how many soldiers are now besieged in the two bases. If anything, it is even harder to be certain about facts inside the bases than outside on the streets. Large-scale transfers of troops take place every day. Like the final Americans, other Western soldiers awaiting evacuation keep themselves busy by packing up. Those who are ready are moved across to the harbour to be close to the ships.

The tens of thousands of empty containers in which the blue helmet city arrived in Somalia have been stacked in long rows. Between these metal hulks runs a complicated system of narrow, draughty paths, which lead past the various UN contingents to the heart of the base.

Dizzy from the noise and ever more thirsty, I plough my way through the loose sand between the containers in search of a UN spokesman to interview. I am not the only one to be lost in this burning labyrinth: the entire UN population seems to have lost its way too. Soldiers and civilians scurry past with rifles and forms in their hands, looking for each other. I ask them the way to their spokesman.

'Is he still here, then?' and 'The last time I saw one on CNN it was a Korean, I think, but I don't know where the Koreans are now,' are the kinds of answers I get. Some take a helpful look round a pile of containers to see if there happens to be a spokesman lurking behind them. It looks like I'm in for a long trek.

With my tongue hanging out, I'm beginning to think I've discovered a system in the layout of the base. The blue helmet contingents are camped according to country of origin on their own plots of ground, marked out by sandbags and containers. The poorer the country, the closer to the beset outer wall of the base its contingent is placed.

Close to the Turkish Gate, at a noisy crossroads where helicopters whip up even more sand than the wind and where trucks and jeeps rattle through blaring their horns, you find the Bangladeshis. Their national flag flutters from an electricity mast planted in the middle of their plot, and the pyjamas which Bangladeshi soldiers wear in their free time are hung out to air on the guy ropes. Tiny bantam chickens pick their way between the tents, pecking vainly at the sand. A blue-helmeted Bangladeshi carefully waters red pepper plants in a vegetable plot. He pours from a bottle of mineral water, crates of which are stacked next to the tents. He nods to me with great affability, but speaks not a word of English.

Long before I discover the Indians camped behind the next row of containers, I can smell their simmering curries. I peep through the flaps of a tent and see a gilded statue of Shiva set up on an altar, complete with burning joss sticks and rice offerings. Shiva appears again on the face of a clock propped against a canvas wall. The hands are set to Indian Standard Time.

A huge Sikh in a blue turban peels potatoes and tosses them into pans steaming over a wood fire. He thinks the spokesman may be Nepalese, but can't tell me where he speaks.

The Nepalese know nothing about it. They are extremely courteous Gurkhas and their sector consists of three tents. They do, however, proudly inform me that they are about to move to Port Base, where the Americans have entrusted the task of guarding the gates to themselves and the Egyptians.

I march off, infected by their enthusiasm, and soon find myself feeling like a visitor to a world exhibition. Camped in another sandpit are the Zimbabweans, no doubt about it. Tourist posters of 'Beautiful Victoria Falls' are stuck to walls of their tents, while on bedside tables beside camp beds stand mahogany statues of African gods. Further on I find the Egyptians, in a camp hung with framed portraits of President Mubarak. Posters of Cheops and Abu Simbel by Night are pinned up around dining tables and in latrine cubicles. The sandy floors of the tents are covered with hand-knotted carpets.

An Egyptian soldier hangs over a pile of sandbags and stares wistfully at his Zimbabwean neighbours. Some of them are taking a shower (behind a waist-high wooden screen) from a pipe sticking out of a suspended water butt.

'Congratulations on being appointed to guard the airport,' I say.

'What do you mean, congratulations? It will be the death of us!' howls the Egyptian. 'Ooooooh! These Somali people, always making trouble, trouble, trouble!'

He bursts into an unstoppable catalogue of woe. This is a very, very unhappy Egyptian. He was a military reservist, plucked from his job as a teacher in a village outside Cairo and sent to Somalia. When he arrived there was a brief moment when it looked like he might be allowed to go home immediately: Egypt was threatening to withdraw her troops from the mission if the UN did not come up with some back pay fast.

'But the money appeared and Egypt signed up again. My UN tour still has ten months to go and it is still another five months before my turn for R&R in Mombasa. Here it is no life for a man.' His eyes have become watery. 'Now I have gate duty, I will probably never make it to the Florida.'

I can find no words of comfort and so take my leave. Resuming my journey, I cross the small camps that belong to the Moroccans and the Nigerians and then find Botswana, whose government has presented Somalia with a platoon of Bushmen. These are the smallest blue helmets I have so far encountered and have ritual scars etched in their cheeks. They sit in a row on the sand in front of their tents and polish their boots.

Closer to the heart of Embassy I find the Malaysians. A pile of rolled-up mats stands ready for the next of their five daily prayer sessions. The spicy aroma of krètek cigarettes hangs between the tents.

Romanians, Koreans and Argentinians lie on their beds and fill in their UN discharge forms. In the container corridor which takes me past the Namibians – who turn out to be big blond guys, much to my surprise – I run into a troop of Turkish soldiers. With their camp beds and cooking gear under their arms they are en route to their new location. The UN has appeased the Turks, who were threatening to leave the mission, by appointing a Turkish general as UN Force Commander. His American predecessor has already gone home. The promotion of the Turks in the military hierarchy means a new camp in one of the base's better neighbourhoods.

When I spot bath towels with 'I love Olivia Newton-John' and 'No Worries, Mate' flapping on the line, I know that I've found just such a neighbourhood. This is where the Australians live and goddammit if there aren't a couple of sun-hats with corks dangling from the brim. This is the business centre for the base: Western countries mainly send technical and logistical specialists, whose contributions to Continue Hope are made from offices, garages and workshops. Australians man the booking office for the UN shuttle helicopters and New Zealanders run the stores in the UN depots.

The closer you get to the heart of the UN city, the more luxurious the accommodation becomes. There is now barely a tent to be seen: Western soldiers have brought their own facilities with them from home. In these white neighbourhoods the soldiers are less encamped than in residence, with neat rows of air-conditioned aluminium billets, complete with running water: I can hear toilets flushing. Third World troops can only long for such things. Their tent areas out by the wall are ghettos by comparison, where the sand lies thick on the mattresses, where temperatures rise to unbearable heights, and where the toilets are holes in the ground. In the absence of an accommodation service, there is bitter wrangling over any plot coming vacant close to the centre. Especially coveted are those sites whose former owners have left without bothering to dismantle their aluminium houses.

I pass broad-shouldered Norwegians in sports gear, pumping iron in a shiny fitness facility shipped out from Norway. Packing cases stand ready and waiting in the corner. Further on I find the remnants of the German contingent, in swimming trunks, stretched out on the bonnets of their white jeeps. This may be the last time they sunbathe outside Aideed's Garage, the camp bar: their ship for home has already berthed. Satisfaction reigns.

'*Die Somalis sind ja crazy,*' a peeling Berliner lazily assures me, '*Und die Amerikaner auch.*'

Two Irish soldiers, drinking at a folding table by the entrance, shout, 'Hear, hear!' and raise their beer glasses in a toast. The Germans call for more beer. The man on bar duty opens the bottles with his teeth.

'It costs 60,000 Deutsche Mark an hour to have us lying around here,' says a German sergeant called Joachim, who is glistening with sun block. Pure boredom has driven them to work out the precise cost of German participation in this UN mission.

'We were based at the most boring place in the whole of Somalia, as far as possible from the front, somewhere on the Ethiopian border. Bonn wanted to be part of this mission, but didn't want to risk German lives.'

The Germans remain under German command, even when in UN service. 'Our government does not allow us to behave like soldiers. We have to be aid workers. This is the first time since the Second World War that German fighting units have appeared beyond German borders, so we are not to scare anybody. In the beginning we dug lots of wells. But we gave that up pretty quick, because the buckets and pumps were all stolen before we could properly donate them to the villagers. The rest of our time in Somalia we've spent raking the sand in our camp.'

Maybe the Germans, hiding away under their own orders in a quiet corner of the country, have not added much to the UN mission, but the 700 men of the Canadian airborne unit contributed even less. During their short stay (they have been already withdrawn from Somalia) they managed to make the clans even more ill-disposed towards the UN than before. 'The Canadians beat a Somali teenager to death. Just a kid, who got caught creeping into the Canadian camp.' After this killing it took UN officials a lot of time and careful diplomacy to get the clans back to the negotiating table.

The Canadians then had their offer to help in Croatia politely refused by the UN in New York. They went anyway, and are now under investigation by a Canadian disciplinary commission: for misconduct while guarding a Croatian psychiatric hospital, where they allegedly abused and tortured the patients.

'Look, there go a few more useful mission members.' Joachim nods towards a row of Italian tanks, rumbling past Aideed's Garage. No blue helmets on view here, and no military crew cuts. Gelled hairstyles poke out of the turrets. Astride each barrel is perched an Italian, the gun protruding between the thighs like a grotesque phallus. Uniforms, tight. Sunglasses, Ray Ban. Belts, stuffed with pistols. 'To look like *Miami Vice*,' sneers Joachim.

The 2,400 Italians have caused more problems than any other national contingent in Somalia. They finally banished themselves from the UN bases before their colleagues could throw them out. To start with they were not even invited to take part in Continue Hope. Italy, the former colonial power, had been supplying weapons to the regime of President Siad Barre (since ousted by the clans) up to the very last minute. 'This is not the best moment for the Italians to come to Somalia,' said an American spokesman in Mogadishu at the start of the operation. 'They do not have a good reputation here.'

Boutros-Ghali also suggested that the Italians should stay away from Somalia and instead reinforce their contingent to the undermanned UN mission in Mozambique. Italy promptly threatened to withdraw the forces it already had there, if the UN refused to accept Italian participation in Somalia: Italy wanted *per se* to be back in its old colony.

'Inviting yourself to the party and then complaining when you don't like it, that's typically Italian,' thinks Joachim. Three Italians were shot dead in Mogadishu during a UN attempt to disarm the locals: 'All Italy in mourning. I saw it on CNN: 15,000 people came to the funerals in Rome. Everyone weeping and kissing the coffins.'

Immediately the solemnities were concluded, Rome demanded to be given command of Continue Hope. They would understand the Somali soul better than anyone else and be able to persuade their 'old friends' in Somalia's elite to make peace. But the Italians did not get the command and since then have refused to co-operate with the UN. They remained in Somalia, but in their own camp, which stands in Aideed's part of town. Other blue helmet contingents do not dare venture up there.

'The Italians have openly done a deal with our greatest enemy, just to spite the UN.' According to Joachim, the UN base very rarely hears anything now from Checkpoint Pasta (their name for the Italian free state in downtown Mogadishu). UN orders are no longer sent there, since they would just be ignored. Boutros-Ghali's attempt to get the Italian Commander removed for insubordination failed for the same reason. 'Italy decides for herself who leads Italian troops,' cried the Italian Minister of Defence, appealing to national sovereignty.

Nobody is happy with the Italian presence, but the Nigerians bear a special grudge. 'The Italians pay Aideed protection money to leave them alone, only they won't admit it. Our suspicions were confirmed when a Nigerian unit had to take over an Italian post in the city. Aideed's men promptly arrived to collect their money, as was the custom, but the Nigerians sent them away, arguing that the UN is neutral and can't justify deals with individual clans. Whereupon they were attacked and seven Nigerians were killed.'

All the contingents approved by the Germans have either left or are leaving soon. Take the lads from the French Foreign Legion, who used often to drop into Aideed's Garage. They certainly liked to party, says Joachim. But then they were withdrawn overnight by the French government, whose concerns had shifted to developments in Rwanda. Tutsi rebels were threatening to win their war against the Hutu regime. France was supporting the Hutus. Militarily too, now.

'Isn't it a bit feeble of Germany to turn its back on Continue Hope at the very moment that the reconstruction of Somalia is supposed to begin?' I ask.

'Sure, and be the only ones to stay on with a bunch of Third World troops?' comes the indignant response.

'So, the mission has been all very professional up to now, has it?' I throw back. 'The Germans sweeping out their camp? The Canadians beating up children? The Italians colluding with the enemy? The Americans waging war against the very people the UN is trying to make peace with? The French just deserting the mission?'

'All true,' says Joachim, 'but at least the Western troops had nice gear with them. The Pakistanis and the Indians who are staying have nothing and they're not trained up to our standard. If we stayed, we'd be dependent on them for our safety. The Indians are already in charge of the interior, and the Pakistanis are going to get Mogadishu.' He nods towards the Irish patrons of Aideed's Garage. 'Ask them. They're already under "Indian protection", whatever that may be.'

'Well, not exactly,' the Irish protest. 'Formally perhaps, but in practice we avoid the Indians like the plague and protect ourselves. We don't listen to Indian orders.' They are the only Western troops who have signed up for another six months of Somalia. There is a small Irish transport unit based up in Baidoa, 150 kilometres beyond Mogadishu. Surrounded by

Indians, they add with disgust. 'Relying on them would be suicide. They haven't a clue. We get Somalis creeping round our camp every week. They just wander straight through the Indian cordon.

'And we'd rather have nothing to do with them socially. Sometimes we can't avoid it and we have to go into their camp for something or other. They always come hustling us with their disgusting sweet tea and hot snacks, even at seven o'clock in the morning.

'They're bums. If they see a white man, they immediately start begging, for our boots, for our flak-jackets, for our ballpoint pens. They don't have anything themselves?

'The Indian officers call their men peasants, which they probably are. Plucked from the paddy fields and given a uniform. When an officer goes for a shit, he is followed by a soldier with a bowl of water, so that when Your Man has finished he can wash his hands without waiting. You wouldn't get an Irish soldier to do that.'

When one of the Irish claims that the Indians are responsible for the plague of flies up in Baidoa, I feel it is time to take my leave.

If I am right, and the location of a blue helmet contingent within Embassy Base reflects the economic state of their country of origin, then Pakistan must be bankrupt. The Pakistanis run the UN field posts and bivouac on roofs and behind piles of sandbags in the city. Thirty-four Pakistani soldiers have already died. Inside the base I encounter a few of their officers.

'Rise to distinction. Join the Pakistani Army' says the poster on the door of Captain Ponnapra's office. I am the guest of the Thundering Thirteen, renowned and respected throughout Pakistan, the Captain assures me. Stars, medals, stripes and a badge of crossed sabres besiege the blue UN emblem on his jacket. He points them out one by one. 'This one means I can parachute, this one is for completing a mountaineering training, and this one says I can fly helicopters.'

Pakistan and other poor countries have sent the cream of their officer corps to this, the largest and most expensive UN operation ever. In such an international line-up, the Third World is presenting itself in its Sunday best. Ponnapra's peers from Bangladesh and India, with whom he shares this aluminium office, are the same kind of richly decorated apparition as he is himself. I melt from the Omar Sharif effect of their presence. They stride through the base like Maharajas. Spotless, tall and athletic, with aristocratic moustaches, they are all graduates of foreign military academies. They address me in upper-class English, spiced with their own oriental accents. On the wooden floor of the office lie well-beaten, hand-knotted carpets. On the wall hangs a glass case full of silverware, gilded bowls and ceremonial swords: the trophy cabinet of the Thundering Thirteen. One inscription records the regiment's courageous contribution to the India–Pakistan wars, while another informs me that last month the Thirteen won the blue helmet basketball competition, beating Saudi Arabia in the final.

Anyone of any Pakistani, Bangladeshi or Indian significance in Mogadishu assembles in Ponnapra's office to meet me. My visit is greatly appreciated, that much is clear. These contingents receive precious little attention from the media, what there is being no doubt unwelcome and patronizing. The officers now sit on Ponnapra's desk, legs dangling and hand in hand as convention requires, noisily sucking on sweets despatched from the home front.

Back in the sub-continent, officers like these have been killing each other in border disputes ever since Partition in 1947. Here domestic rivalries have been shelved in pursuit of a higher goal: recognition of their several military capacities by the Western states who call the shots within the UN.

Although the Pakistan army has already done its UN duty on low-profile missions like Papua New Guinea and Cyprus, being part of Somalia, an operation set up by the US Army, the world's largest and most advanced military machine, marks a step up on the international ladder. Pakistan's chances of leading part of the UN mission to Bosnia have been riding on their performance here in Somalia. Events have gone against them.

'When we finally get the chance to show the West what we are worth, they all leave,' growls Ponnapra. 'I was really looking forward to working with the US Army and its Western allies. I thought I could learn from it. Well, I have certainly been impressed by their weapons and vehicles, but not by their courage and military qualities. The Americans have bungled the job here and most other Westerners have never been outside the camp gates. While we, who have remained true to the mission, are going to pay the price. Because obviously we are going to fail. With less and less budget, without Western weapons and Western logistics, all we can hope for is that the clans will soon leave us alone. The idea that we, on our own, will be able to erect a whole new Somalia is of course an illusion.'

The fact that they are staying on after the American departure has not made these Asians the humanitarian heroes of the UN, but rather the laughing stock of the whole operation. This cynical contradiction has not eluded Ponnapra. 'I know what they call us, you know: Third World troops. The arrogance of it! India, Pakistan and Bangladesh happen to be just about the only countries in this whole operation who have real war experience. The other contingents only know war from Hollywood films.'

'Rambo!' giggles one of the officers.

'The Muscles from Brussels!' cries another.

'I have personally put down a popular insurrection on the Burmese border,' says a Bangladeshi.

'And I riots in Kashmir!' states an Indian.

'I have managed three floods. In one of them I saved the lives of 20,000 people by presenting them with the rations of my own men. We have also given up part of our pay so that the victims could build new houses. *Chai!*' Ponnapra snaps his fingers to summon a soldier whose sole task in Somalia is to keep his officers constantly supplied with fresh tea. The young soldier squats in a corner, attending a silver tea pot on a charcoal burner. He serves me tea in a porcelain cup and salutes. The tea is milky and cloyingly sweet, exactly as it is in Pakistan.

It is not just in Somalia that India, Pakistan and Bangladesh are providing the lion's share of the combat troops. This year 90,000 UN soldiers are serving in fourteen different peace missions and the overwhelming majority of them come from the UN's poorest Member States. For poor countries, peace-keeping is a lucrative business. At home soldiers cost money, but as blue helmets they generate income, around $1,000 per soldier per month. Most soldiers from rich countries receive the UN allowance directly, but the governments of poor countries generally put the proceeds in their own pockets. Blue helmets have thus become an export product, although their governments may have to wait dangerously long for equipment and reimbursement. In Kuwait, for example, British soldiers clear mines with British detectors, while detectorless Bangladeshis do the same job by prodding the ground with sticks. 'Boom!' says Ponnapra. 'One after the other.'

UN soldiers from poor countries often have to scrounge

together their kit. If they are allowed to go to Bosnia soon, 3,000 Pakistanis will get at least a winter coat from the German Defence Ministry. They can probably borrow some ambulances and generators from other rich Member States. In other words: the West is providing the cannons, the Third World the fodder.

'Western countries are selective in what they are prepared to do for the UN. We are not. We give the UN carte blanche: do what you want with us, we don't mind. We are ready to die for the UN if need be. Here too, when we lost twenty-four soldiers at one go during a disarming operation, it did not occur to us to say No to any more off-base service, let alone to abandon the mission,' says Ponnapra.

Willing as they are to man the front line in even the most dangerous UN operations, combat troops from poor countries are a high-risk group. Cuts are being made in their insurance cover:

### UN pays out more for rich dead than poor dead

London – The compensation paid out for blue helmets killed during peace missions is more than four times higher for Western countries than for developing countries. Since the end of 1992, the UN have paid $85,000 for every dead UN soldier from the industrialized world, while the average for dead Third World soldiers is $19,500.

The difference can be explained by the fact that UN compensation levels are based on national legislation. 'Because compensation levels for death and serious injury are relatively low in developing countries, the payments made to countries like France and Britain are much higher than those

made to India, Pakistan and Bangladesh,' said a
UN spokesman.

(Jane's Defence Weekly, no. 1, 1995)

As a farewell gift, I am given a handful of sunflower seeds
to nibble and a T-shirt (Pakistani cotton) bearing a map of
Africa and the words 'Somalia '94'.

'Only Allah can still save this mission,' says Ponnapra as he
escorts me out. 'Perhaps He will do it when the Westerners
have left. We are Moslems, just like the Somalis.'

I don't give the Captain much chance. In a recent speech
General Aideed, the archenemy of the UN in Somalia,
announced, 'Pakistanis are poor Moslems, as we are, but the
great difference between the Pakistanis and ourselves is that
they take orders from the Americans and we do not.'

## VI

Bare-chested gents relax under parasols branding cans of
beer, while others sit round the white tables sipping tropical-
looking concoctions. Trickles of condensation drip seduct-
ively from the glasses on to their naked thighs. Just audible
above the drone of the generator, is Julio Iglesias. I have
stepped round a pile of sandbags and straight into a holiday
brochure. On a small square of sand, wedged between the
containers, stands the Classica, the cocktail bar for UN personnel. A board bids me 'Welcome' and announces the newest
attraction: popcorn straight from the machine. And three
nights a week, a film on a big screen (which is now flapping
wildly in the up-draught from circling helicopters). Tonight:
*Dennis the Menace.*

All the tables are taken so it must be Happy Hour. Everything, customers included, is covered in a thin layer of sand. The Classica's managers, three young Israelis, have taken on two Somalis just to flick sand off their stock of drinks. They rinse off cans of Pepsi-Cola and beer in a bucket of water before putting them into the fridge, but customers are still given a couple of sheets of toilet paper with every purchase to give the rims another wipe. The swirling desert is quite able to force its way in through the fridge doors.

The bar also functions as a duty-free shop. The Israelis have the merchandise shipped in from Tel Aviv. Blue helmets pay duty-free prices, just like at Heathrow or Gatwick. Here, however, the sale is done straight from the containers in which the goods entered the country. One is reserved for bar customers and is filled with alcohol, cigarettes and nuts. Blue helmets walk in, serve themselves and pay on the way out to the tables. Other containers look like bargain basements, offering everything from ballpoints to shampoo, table fans, deckchairs and combs.

Julio Iglesias has finished. Now it is Bruce Springsteen belting out 'Born in the USA' from duty-free stereo speakers, a friendly gesture to the group of American soldiers who have just wandered in to rummage through a collection of T-shirts. There is one with 'Mogadishu, the best vacation spot' on offer for only $12. Three for $30.

I eavesdrop on a noisy dispute between the Israeli at the checkout, a young guy with long, blond frizzy hair, and Zimbabwean blue helmets. The Zimbabweans are trying to haggle over the price of a bottle of gin, just as they would do at home.

'Fifteen dollars! You are a rip-off, sir!' cries one of the Zimbabweans with heartfelt conviction.

'Yes. And you're a fucking native,' mutters the Israeli wearily.

I also spot a bit of fraternization: a couple of Saudi blue

helmets are buying in trays of Maccabee beer from the Israelis.

A squad of Nigerians, just back from patrol, trudge on to the terrace, sweating and thirsty, with handkerchiefs over their mouths to keep out the dust. Automatic weapons hang from their drooping shoulders. They shuffle into the drinks container and emerge gulping down cold cans of Pepsi. They've also stocked up on cartons of cigarettes for their next tour of the city.

'I don't believe it! You still alive?' I turn round and look into the face of a total stranger, a blond moustache in his forties. His hair is stiff with dust. The keyboard of the laptop on his knee grates from the sand.

'Big Bruce is the name,' he says in a strong London accent. 'Freelance businessman. What are you drinking?'

Big Bruce has seen me arrive in Mogadishu. He lives in a container bang next to the runway. 'I could see you coming down the aircraft steps through my bedroom window. You looked completely dazed. It reminded me of a doctor from the International Red Cross who came in one day, just like you, first time he'd ever set foot in Mogadishu. Before anyone had time to warn him, he'd wandered out through the gates and was standing on the side of the street waving at the Somali cars in the hope that one of them was a taxi. One of them bounced to a stop and the idiot got in. "That's the last we'll see of him," I thought. But later I heard that the driver had taken him to the Red Cross HQ in the city, but then demanded $2,000 for the ride. The doctor threw him a handful of loose change and told him he should look for a stupid tourist if he really wanted to cheat someone. The row heated up. A whole crowd got involved and followed him into the building screaming. The Red Cross people went white as sheets and dived under their desks. "They've all got machine guns under those robes and you're standing there arguing with them. Are you crazy! Pay them!" they yelled at him.'

Before Big Bruce could run out on the tarmac and stop me committing a similar folly, he saw that the Belgian, and then John, were already saving me.

'You'll be staying at the Al Sahafi then? Expensive, isn't it? You could live very comfortably in one of our containers for half the price. There are still a few empty ones down by the runway. A lot of my colleagues have already quit Mogadishu. There's less and less to earn from this mission. The rich troops are all going home.'

The full moon shines down on the graveyard for crashed MiG fighters and old combat helicopters which begins straight behind my container. Stray cats and ibises flecked with oil forage together through crumpled cockpits and beneath undercarriages. The wrecks have been dumped on top of each other, higgledy-piggledy. You can read 'I love Mom + Beer' scrawled on a broken wing and 'Joe loving his Samantha from far far away' on the pointed nose of a MiG. Big Bruce contemplates the mountain of scrap with the eye of a critical buyer.

'Wrap it in cling-film, ship it to Europe and flog it as modern art,' he decides.

He's got a nose for business, has Bruce. He belongs to a legion of modern camp followers, privateers who swarm into disaster zones in the wake of UN peace missions, looking for anything going. I hear some of them pottering about in the pre-fab kitchen tucked in between our containers: this evening, they and their rivals will patch up their differences over UN contracts round the poker table.

Port, the UN base around the airport and harbour, lies right on the Indian Ocean, in a shimmering sand hollow drenched in leaked kerosene. I had noticed the containers alongside the runway, but never guessed that they were used as a sort of caravan park. With a few clever tricks, the UN contractors have turned their 3,000 kilo steel boxes into snug living quarters, 2 metres high and plastered with photos of ladies' bums. Even more up-front are the PCs, diligently humming away on the tables, from which the privateers submit their tenders to the UN.

We hire these immobile homes from a one-man catering business, a Brit, who came to Somalia twelve months ago for his clients, a team of Russian helicopter pilots, themselves UN contractors. He feeds and houses the Russians in three neat rows of aluminium pre-fabs. Privateers wanting to eat at his establishment and make use of his shower facilities (for a price, of course) merely comb the UN base for a discarded container, talk a friendly crane driver into setting it up next to the Russians, and then move in. The result is a camp which in turn attracts other adventurers, long or short term, seeking their fortunes in this war.

In the moonlight I can see the silhouettes of UN patrols, scurrying over the sand dunes in search of Somali infiltrators. A Hercules comes in low over the sea and prepares to land. We are sitting so close to the runway that I instinctively pull in my legs as the wheels touch down. A platoon of Indonesian blue helmets emerge from the cargo hold and a platoon of New Zealanders, almost all Maoris, climb in. They are going on R&R. The amusement factory in Mombasa is still running on full throttle. I am constantly seeing soldiers returning, still green from their last night at the Florida disco. They ride back to their tents, somewhere out in the sand, in tanks filled with wooden souvenir carvings.

With his hair still wet from the shower, one of my Russian neighbours comes out of his cabin with a banjo under his arm.

He sinks to the sand at my feet and bursts into a melancholy ballad, complete with fluttering eyelashes.

'He is singing about the perils of the Zuiderzee,' translates Bruce helpfully.

A lurid procession of builders, mine-clearers, latrine-diggers and odd-job men files past on its way to the world's wars. New life has been breathed into the old profession of camp follower ever since the end of the Cold War, when Western ministries of defence were ordered to economize. Expenditure reviews revealed that the recruitment and training of soldiers were major items, and that after their expensive training the majority of men were mainly occupied with feeding, washing, moving, housing and administrating each other. By bringing in competitive private businesses to do all the work not directly related to war, ministers could trim back their armies to the essence: i.e. combat units.

The Gulf War opened many eyes, especially those in the Pentagon, to another significant benefit of privatization: the use of private companies served to soothe public opinion. The more private contractors go off to war, the fewer of 'our boys' have to go. And the less trouble the average tax-paying American has with American involvement.

During Desert Storm there had been grumbling. The public saw hundreds of thousands of soldiers, most of them American boys, being stowed into transport planes bound for Baghdad. Your average Joe and his missus assumed that all these kids were bound for the front. In reality most of them would never even see the Gulf War, let alone run any risk of dying in it. The number of soldiers sent into Desert Storm to do the washing, butter the bread and fill in the forms far exceeded the number sent out there to fight. This large war actually required more support units than the US Army was able to mobilize. Private assistance was hired in out of necessity. To the satisfaction of both parties, it would appear.

When the Gulf War was over, the Pentagon invited contractors to submit competitive tenders for America's thirteen ongoing overseas military missions. The winners were Brown & Root Services Corp. out of Houston, Texas. Their tender may not have been the lowest, but it was written by a retired US Army colonel who knew how a war is conducted. The value added by Brown & Root to the American military lay in the CVs it would demand from potential employees: they had to be fully trained war veterans, used to keeping themselves alive under dangerous conditions and capable of screwing the machinery of war together under fire if needs be.

Three months after the end of the Gulf War, the lucrative collaboration between Defence and Brown & Root was up and running. In December 1992 they captured Somalia together. A team of burly construction workers marched in with the American invasion force. Before the US Army had found its way out of the harbour and airport, the men from Brown & Root were already at work on the quays and runways with cranes and concrete mixers.

'Ruined control towers, crumbling wharves, runways full of mortar holes, no water, no electricity. Within a day we had repaired the bulk of it and laid a complete sewage system for the marine fraternity into the bargain,' says 'Butch' Baker, a Brown & Root man and one of my neighbours. 'Within two days we had fixed up water and light and by the time the first food convoys drove out of the gates (that we had repaired), which was the next day, we had made up the beds for the soldiers.'

Every stretch of sand levelled and provided with water, electricity and sewers by Brown & Root meant that more invasion troops could land. 'All the battalions had to do was hoist their colours and hang up a few washing lines,' boasts Butch.

Recruiting staff for this invasion force had been a pushover for Brown & Root management. Unemployed Vietnam veterans, of whom Butch is one, had lined up on the Texas sidewalk and begged for jobs. With a few hundred of their own people and 16,000 Somali workers, Brown & Root is now by far the largest employer in Somalia.

More than 200 contractors, large and small, feed on the crumbs dropped by this king of construction. The small fry scarcely get a look in with the US Army, but UN contracts are well worth the effort. The UN, which has to conduct ever more complex peace missions with ever smaller budgets, farms out as many jobs as it can to the private sector. Entrepreneurs, with little more than a PC and no overheads, are far cheaper than blue helmets. This year, in Somalia alone, there are $166.5 million to be earned by contractors. In cash. There are no banks left in Somalia.

### The battle for UN business

In 1994 the UN spent $1.4 billion on, amongst other things, food, transport, computers and telephones for peace missions. Unicef, the UNHCR and other humanitarian UN organizations paid out $2.4 billion on food aid, tents, vaccination, drinking water facilities and the transport for these items. In 1994 America was top of the list of UN suppliers with sales of $737 million, followed by Italy with $230 million and the UK with $229 million.

American companies received 37% of the UN budget for peace missions, but only 12% of the UN budgets for humanitarian intervention. European companies have an advantage as suppliers for the UN's humanitarian agencies, such as the UNHCR or the World Food Programme, since most of these are based in Europe.

(AP, 12 June 1996)

It doesn't take long to get used to aircraft landing and taking off right next to the bed. In the morning I am usually the last to wake and find myself alone in the container village with the Somali cleaners who are included in the rent. Squatting in the shadows cast by the wings of the crashed MiGs and chattering away in high voices, the women wash our sheets in buckets. I am already melting in just a T-shirt at eight o'clock in the morning, but these women are concealed from the tops of their heads to the tips of their toes under several layers of flapping cloth. The vividness of the colours, set against the soft beige of the Somali desert, almost hurts my eyes.

Some of the women speak a smattering of English through their veils. When they hear I come from Holland, they are excited. Holland is popular in Somalia. It is virtually the only country where you can still get asylum as a Somali.

'Her son, and hers, and her husband and all her sons, all in Holland,' says a woman in delight as she wrings out a sheet. Her own son has been given asylum in Burgenupzome, she tells me. I try to puzzle it out. 'Burgenupzome,' she repeats, and suddenly I get a flash of the elegant harbour at Bergen op Zoom. 'Do you know him? His name is Mohammed.' Tomorrow she will give me a letter for her son. She never hears anything from him, because no post has been delivered in Somalia for years.

★

It is a good thing the privateers have provided the UN bases with satellite TV, because now I can watch CNN to see what is happening out on the streets of Mogadishu. Ever since I moved into my steel box, I have met nobody who is involved in the war raging outside the gates or who is even interested in it.

In the mornings I see convoys of blue helmets from Bangladesh and Nigeria riding out of the gate in armoured vehicles. They rumble off to the city with gun barrels protruding in all directions, like pins from a pincushion. In the evenings I see them returning from work, tired, thirsty and covered with dust. They wash and withdraw to their tents until the following morning.

I sometimes ask them what it looks like outside. They see nothing but crazy people killing each other, they tell me. Who these people are and why they are acting so crazy, that they don't know. Nor do they care, since they are not allowed to meddle in anything anyway.

I can learn little more from the privateers. From the contracts they're chasing, I can at least guess how the UN is doing on any one day. Yesterday, for example, Bruce put in a bid for some masonry work up at the Mogadishu prison. There are holes in the wall which need patching up. So apparently Chief Commissioner Ali and his men are managing to arrest the occasional villain.

Port and Embassy are about a kilometre apart as the crow flies, but the only surviving link is by helicopter. UN shuttle buses, still possible at the start of the mission, have become too dangerous. The Somalis are now at war with the UN. Shuttle choppers, sprayed UN white, rise every fifteen minutes, flown by our Russians. The bus-stop is right in front of our doors, so my neighbours can get straight out of bed and take off. Inside there are benches with room for about twenty, strapped in and facing each other. The commuters sit in camouflage fatigues with automatic weapons on their knees, or (if they are privateers) with laptops.

The contractors are fully aware that 'there's cash in chaos'. The failed attempts to disarm the locals made by UN troops under US command proved to be a goldmine. UN contingents that had been spread out all over Somalia now fled back to the safety of the UN bases in Mogadishu for fear of Somali reprisals. The privateers who had built the blue helmet camps in the interior were now hired to dismantle them. They were joined by a freelance undertaker, still running his practice from a warehouse at the airport. Here he lays out dead blue helmets before they go into the body bags.

In the morning the contractors gather in the office of the UN Procurement Department, right at the heart of Base Embassy, and scan the notice board for new jobs. The departure of Western troops in the wake of the US Army is also good for turnover. Most of the contingents let freelancers dismantle and pack up their camps. But the troops that are due to replace them will all come from Africa and Asia. 'People who come here to earn money for themselves. They dig their own latrines and put what they save on the budget in their pockets,' says Bruce from bitter experience.

But the contractors' hope is that one day, and soon, the job pinned up on the wall will be the reconstruction of Somalia itself. The first millions of aid dollars have already been flown in and a slice of this cake is the main thing that keeps Big Bruce and his mates hanging around. 'If the UN ever wants to get a government off the ground here, then they're going to need a parliament building. The old one is in ruins. Palace, ministries, mosques, there's nothing left, except maybe half a wall next to a mountain of rubble. All has to be rebuilt. There is no point at the moment: every brick, every nail would be nicked.'

Until the reconstruction millions start to flow, there is nothing to which my versatile neighbours are not willing to turn their hands: malfunctioning toilet cisterns in UN offices, flapping metal sheeting on canteen roofs, garbage collection, cleaning UN hospitals, fitting extra wall sockets, repairing water pipes and kerbstones. And for anything they can't do themselves, they hire in Somali sub-contractors and workers from the hundreds who stand outside the gates begging for work.

To the blue helmets, the Mogadishu privateers are 'the gladiators' and the name is well chosen. The UN bases, sandy spaces ringed by defensive walls, are the arena through which they stomp in their shorts and short sleeves, brushing aside any blue helmets who get in their way. Their tattooed arms hang wide from their heavy bodies to accommodate their bulging muscles. The gladiators don't give a damn about being stuck in Somalia. 'As long as they pay, we stay,' say Bruce and Butch, and bang their fists together in comradeship.

'Offer them a contract and the gladiators will go win a war for you,' say the blue helmets with awe. Bruce, pensioned off by the British SAS, fought in the Falklands. Butch Baker, Vietnam veteran, worked for Brown & Root during the Gulf War. Karl, another container camp neighbour, is ex-US Special Forces, while our landlord served as a commando with the British army in Northern Ireland. Most of the privateers have the same career profile: into the army at eighteen, pensioned off by their respective armed forces at around forty. With a meagre pension and drilled in a profession for which there is little demand back on Civvie Street, Brown & Root or going freelance to war are a real way out. Alternatives for the average veteran are scarce and poorly paid: used to the clatter of weapons and trained to kill, the best they can expect from society is security work in a department store or guarding armoured money transports for a bank. And social isolation, if it has since been decided that the war they once fought in was wrong.

Marriages usually collapse when they leave the army. 'After twenty years in the commandos, all that hoovering round my feet drove me crazy. And I drove my ex crazy too,' says Bruce. After his divorce there was nothing to stop him going back to war, 'but well paid this time'.

'The first thing I did as a freelance was the Gulf War,' says Bruce. 'In Saudi I turned over $18 million in eight months. I then had a seat on the very first plane into Kuwait after the liberation. Worked there six months, just broke even. I'd got there too late. The UN had handed out all the best contracts back in New York, long before the end of Desert Storm. I'm turning over half a million a month here, but if the reconstruction of Somalia ever gets going I could maybe double that.'

Butch, who has been walking up with us, now lets out a loud burp and asks if I happen to fancy a quick screw. No? Then he has to get back to work. With his heavy body tucked into his oil-spattered denim shorts (old cut-off jeans), he rejoins his ten-tonner. Brown & Root have the contract for dismantling and packing up the American army. Every day Butch fills containers with American weapons and transports them down to the ships in the harbour. He props his beer belly behind the wheel, waves and disappears in a cloud of dusty sand and exhaust fumes.

'If he hadn't found work here, he'd be back home beating his wife and kids. No doubt about it. Me too, I should think,' says Bruce.

This morning there's only one UN job pinned up on the

wall at Procurement: the soldiers' canteen at Embassy needs fitting with mortar nets. The more American weapons are packed up and shipped out, the more the Somalis dare to bombard the base. 'If they did it at lunchtime, then Continue Hope would be dead in one blow. With mortar nets stretched over the canteen roof there's at least a chance that projectiles will bounce off before they explode,' explains Bruce.

He goes to collect his $30,000 for unblocking the water supply to the Turkish camp, stuffs the notes casually into his pockets and climbs into his jeep. He drives with one hand, the finger of the other tucked round the trigger of the Beretta which lives in the glove compartment. 'Shoot first, ask questions later' is the Somalia policy of the peace mission's privateers. They keep spray-cans of tear gas ready on the front seat, just for the little bastards who hang around outside the gates.

'Back soon,' cries Bruce, waves goodbye with his gun and roars out through the Turkish Gate into the street. He is going to check whether his Somali sub-contractors have finished patching up the walls of the prison.

Catering for UN soldiers in Somalia is still bringing in millions every month for various entrepreneurs, but dark clouds are gathering. The Sri Lankan kitchen staff at Bogart's Take Away point significantly to the chickens scratching away in the hot sand.

'The more the Westerners disappear, the more poultry we see on the base. Soldiers from poor countries curry them. Asians and Africans think our hamburgers are a waste of money and cook their own dinners.' The Sri Lankans have calculated that this is costing them $5 per soldier per day. The UN pays governments $15 per soldier per day. 'By expecting his soldiers to cook their own dinners, a clever defence minister can make millions a month out of UN missions, while our turnover goes down from six to one thousand dollars a day. Mr Bogart wants to get out of here fast. He is looking for a new mission to sell snacks to.'

The Sri Lankans have been twelve years on the road with the hamburger king. Wherever the US Army descends, a Bogart's will sooner or later arise. Their previous pitch was Saudi Arabia during Desert Storm. A few of the cooks have saved almost enough to get married back in Sri Lanka. Mr Singh, who operates the till, has even managed to get rich and after Somalia he'll go back to Sri Lanka and open a paint shop, which is what he has always wanted.

Photo albums appear. A proud Singh stands next to a Dutch tourist outside a temple in Sri Lanka's holy city of Kandy. Then a photo of a woman with a row of daughters in dresses with lots of pink tulle and white lace.

'Mrs Singh,' says Singh. 'Not seen her for five years. It's always work, work, work for me.'

The Somalia ambitions of David Morris, the Australian caterer, go far beyond feeding blue helmets. He is doing deals worth millions here and a lot of Somalis don't like it. Of all the freelance caterers serving the UN in Somalia, he is the most successful. Rumours about him abound. He is using his time here to set up businesses that various clans run in his name. Long after the UN mission has gone and he and the troops have moved on, money will keep flowing out of Somalia into his pockets. Or so he hopes. In the north of Somalia, for example, he has started a fishing business with partners from a local clan. They catch lobsters and export them across the Gulf of Aden to Saudi Arabia. Morris has provided them with a better boat than the competing clans. He thus has good reason to assume that there is a price on his head, maybe several. His oldest son has already met his end in

Mogadishu. Executed, it must be. Because when the car forced him to pull over, only young Morris was shot, none of the passengers.

Other UN contract caterers have fresh vegetables flown in from Saudi, which is not cheap. Morris uses locally grown produce. A few Somali farmers do still manage to grow something, and by buying up their whole harvest Morris is able to run the most competitive business in town.

When I go to collect locally grown tomatoes with Mark, Morris's English buyer who'd arrived as a freelance photographer, our bodyguards are Cambodian Khmers. Morris discovered them while with the UN mission in Cambodia and brought them to Somalia to protect his shopping convoys. They hang out of the windows and from the flaps at the backs of our three trucks.

We leave Mogadishu on a track that is barely wide enough for the trucks. We roar along just missing the graves in the dried-out shoulder. The dead lie where they fell from hunger and thirst in 1992. They are covered with loose rubble and thorn branches, because under a thin layer of dust the sandy earth of Somalia is as hard as stone. No point trying to dig graves.

We are in the leading truck. Our driver is relying on speed to save us from bandits, who may be lying in ambush behind the withered scrub. The Khmers do not take their fingers off the triggers of their Uzis for a second. With red scarves tied round their foreheads to keep the sweat out of their eyes, they stare through their sights throughout the journey as if in a trance. Morris sends Mark and the Khmers off to his Somali suppliers twice a week, trusting that at least they won't shoot at the vegetable convoy. After all, he is taking virtually their entire crop and for a better price than Somali customers can pay.

Donkey carts are driven off the track in panic as we

approach. A herd of white camels surges backwards and bolts. Their yelling owners set off in pursuit, cloaks flapping round their hips in the hot wind. Garishly painted Somali trucks wait beside the road, belching diesel fumes, hoping to force their way into our convoy. Bonnets are missing, bumpers drag in the dust, doors and windows are riddled with bullet holes: truckers are a popular target for clans. This lot want to take advantage of our Khmer protection, but their vehicles are held together with bits of rope and paperclips and just don't have the power. Besides, the Khmers are professional convoy men. Our driver marshals his trucks like a cowboy rounds up his herd when rustlers are around. He radios the drivers behind to close up and keep bumper to bumper. The old Somali wagons strain to stay in touch, but I watch them in the mirror as they drop back one after the other.

Suddenly, in the middle of the road, there is a man with no legs. We avoid him with difficulty. He stretches out a begging hand.

'Baksheesh! Ciao!' he screams at us. The Italians must have passed this way recently, distributing alms. Mark throws him a tin of processed cheese from his lunch box. For a group of women further on it's a packet of chewing gum. Other beggars almost get themselves crushed under our wheels. They stand their ground in the road, pleading, until we nearly run them over. A child in rags, its eyes screwed up against the dust cloud that we're throwing up, waves a large dagger clutched in its little fist.

With the collars of our flak jackets pulled up as high as they'll go, we drive through a refugee camp. There is nothing to stop a Somali being a refugee and a sniper at the same time, the Khmer driver assures me. The refugees have built upside-down birds' nests to live in. They bend over the branches of thorn bushes and tie them together. Then garbage from the UN camps, old sandbags and flattened cardboard boxes, is used for the walls and roofs. The shelters read 'Kronenbourg Beer', 'Pure Spring Water from Dubai' and 'USA MRE' (Meals Ready to Eat). As far as construction goes, the termite mounds which punctuate this flat landscape are far more solid.

The driver tosses his empty Fanta can out of the window.

'They can build another house with it,' he grins.

We approach an oasis. A rusting tank from the ex-President's collection stands guard at the edge. A huge piece of cloth has been tied to the barrel, beneath which someone has stabled his camel. The children run with the trucks until we pull into the centre of the village and come to a stop between sun-baked mud huts. The Khmers drop from the cabs on to the hot sand and form a nervous cordon around the vehicles, brandishing their Uzis.

Dozens of Somalis have already crept out of their huts and are pressing around us in a thick cloud of dust. The village doctor, seated at a wobbly table under the tree, breaks off his surgery to come and inspect us. He pops the pot of de-worming pills that he prescribes for all his patients into his pocket, out of the way of thieves.

Mark produces a large set of commercial scales from the back of one of the trucks. He sets it up on the ground, while women hasten in from the fields with sacks on their heads. The sacks are marked 'World Food Programme' and once held sugar and flour. Now they contain the harvest. The weighing can only begin when the Mayor, with beard hanging over a dusty white robe, has ceremoniously unfolded his chair and taken his place in front of the scales. He has only recently been appointed to office by the UN.

At his signal the first woman upends her sack over one of

our plastic crates. Lettuces tumble out. A sturdy assistant hoists the full crate up on to the scales.

'Thirteen point two kilos,' cheers the Mayor.

'Thirteen point one,' corrects Mark. Both he and the Mayor mark down the weights on order forms bearing the Morris logo. A sack of lemons is emptied into the next crate.

'Fifteen point eight kilos.' The Mayor rises from his chair to point emphatically at the stripe where the indicator has stopped.

'Fifteen point six,' corrects Mark impassively. And accurately. Even I can see that the Mayor is adding a couple of hundred grams. He tries it with every crate. Mark goes on correcting him, to the obvious irritation of both. After a few more crates the Mayor loses his temper and calls us everything under the sun in Somali. The crowd around us immediately take up the cry and begin to threaten us with their fists. Out of the corner of my eye I see the Khmers rise, as quick and silent as cats, and level their weapons. Only when the Mayor, still grumbling, slides back into his chair, do they slowly drop back to a squatting position.

The full crates disappear into the backs of our trucks; carrots, more lemons, red peppers and an apparently endless stream of lettuce flow from the pickers' sacks.

'Far too much lettuce. We'll never sell it all,' Marks complains quietly to me. 'But we've agreed to take the whole crop.'

The weighing has already taken an hour and a half. Flies crawl up our nostrils and the heat in the square is nauseating. The Mayor sends a couple of women to the nearby well to hoist up some buckets of water. Their feet sink into the mud and the camel shit. They empty the buckets all round the boss's chair in an attempt to dampen the whirling dust.

'Eight point two.' Yet more lettuce.

'Eight point one. You promised tomatoes. Where are the goddamn tomatoes?' snaps Mark irritably.

'Twelve point zero.' Kilos of lettuce.

'Eleven point nine.' Mark is pissed off with it. 'You take over for a bit while I look for something to drink,' he says to me. Before I can protest, he has turned to the Mayor and announced, 'This woman is the boss now!'

The Mayor examines me with such disgust that I get goose bumps right up to my neck.

'Six point five,' he says, testing me out straightaway. It is six point two kilos of lettuce, but I let him get away with it. As far as I am concerned, a few cents more on Morris's bill is not worth a gun battle between the Khmers and the local council.

When we have loaded 1,400 kilos of lettuce and, sure enough, weighed out 250 kilos of tomatoes, the sacks are empty and the trucks are full. The Khmers clamp their left eyes back on to their sights and don't shift their position until we are back in Mogadishu and have driven in through the gates of UN Port Base.

We are still unloading the crates when my British landlord drives up to Morris's warehouse. He theatrically places a mouldy carrot on Mark's desk and waits, exuding triumph, for his reaction.

'Whadissit?' says Mark with the weariness born of experience.

'Rubbish. Money back,' says my landlord.

'Go and find Morris. I've got no money.'

A soldier turns up with another complaint, a New Zealander. 'We don't want any more of those little tomatoes. They're so difficult to cut into quarters.'

'Then cut 'em in half,' says Mark.

'Can't do that, 'cos we serve them in salads and quarters of big tomatoes look nicer than halves of little tomatoes.' The Khmers listen as they loosen their headscarves. They exchange meaningful looks and slap Mark encouragingly on the shoulder before they withdraw to their kampong of huts, built of waste wood next to the warehouse. Cambodian ladies are waiting outdoors with pans, from which unfamiliar smells arise.

'What do you risk your life for? For miserable bastards who moan about the design of their salads,' sighs Mark. And he refers the New Zealander on to the boss.

Three days later I get bad news: the shopping convoy with Mark and the Khmers has run into an ambush. They'd had to brake for a wrecked car in the middle of the track and immediately found themselves under fire from all sides. None of the Khmers has survived. Mark has had his leg shot to pieces. After the attackers had disappeared with the trucks, Mark dragged himself into the road, dizzy from loss of blood. Cars full of foreign aid workers drove past, but instead of stopping they speeded up, afraid that Mark had been put there as bait. He was finally picked up by some Red Cross people, who rushed him to the little UN hospital on the base. An emergency operation and evacuation to England followed. In London they are trying to see if they can save the leg.

For Morris himself, the outcome was even worse. He became a victim of the escalating savings being made by UN Member States at the expense of the Somalia mission:

### Australian businessman murdered in Mogadishu

Nairobi, 30 April 1995 – Australian national David Morris, who was abducted by his creditors in Mogadishu, has been murdered today. The catering firm owned by Morris says that unpaid invoices have caused the drama. David Morris owed Somali traders $2 million. Morris, who had a contract with the United Nations to supply UN troops with fruits and vegetables, was unable to meet his bills, because the United Nations failed to pay invoices worth $20 million. Morris was held by gunmen of a Somali trader who was owed $100,000.

'The problem was not the $100,000 – we could pay that, but you can't just pay one creditor. If you'd just pay one, you'd never get to the airport,' said the managing director of the catering company.                                        (Reuters)

## *VII*

It is growing ever more quiet in the privateers' camp. The reconstruction of Somalia seems not to be happening. Every agreement that the UN concludes with one clan, whatever it may be about, is declared invalid by the other clans as soon as they get wind of it. So the aid dollars are stored away deep in the vaults, while attacks on the UN base become heavier. More promised dollars do not materialize. Now that the Americans are leaving, Brown & Root, Somalia's largest employer, is leaving too. The contractor's Somali staff will soon be back on the streets. Today has seen the first wave of redundancies, and thus the start of Somali revenge: Brown & Root's local truck drivers are taking their fully laden vehicles out of the base with no plans to return. The same is happening with diggers, jeeps and mobile cranes. Meanwhile other Somalis are trying to force their way into the base to lynch their Brown & Root bosses.

Chaos has broken out around UN Port's entrance gates.

Between the Egyptians, who began their new job on the gates today, and the new unemployed on the doorstep, it is immediately war. One of the Egyptians has panicked and shot dead a Somali who was trying to take his gun. The other Somalis have promptly opened fire on the Egyptians. For the moment the rapid reaction of the Gurkhas seems to have calmed the situation. But although the crowd has pulled back from the gates, they have placed mines round the Egyptian sandbags. Urgently required for the Egyptians: dogs trained to locate explosives.

The Somali attacks are Bruce's final stroke of luck on this mission. At the very last moment, just days before he is due to leave, he has managed to land a contract for the sniffer dogs. I find him sweating over his laptop at the kitchen table. 'You've got to be ready for anything when you're self-employed,' he says. 'Listen to this. Egyptians don't like dogs. Dog slobber is unclean for Moslems. If it touches their hands, they have to wash themselves seven times seven times. If a dog dribbles on an Egyptian vehicle, it has to be completely hosed down. They are demanding anti-slobber guarantees in the tender. So what do they expect? Dogs with condoms on their muzzles?'

Picking up his satellite phone, he plunges into his network. Poor connections force him to negotiate at the top of his voice, with privateers from Angola to Saudi, from Lebanon to Cuba. But within half an hour the problem is solved: 'The dogs will only be touched by the British handlers that Contract Unlimited agrees to deliver with them,' Bruce types into his tender with great satisfaction.

This evening the Russians are throwing a leaving party. They have been fired by the UN, which has found cheaper Canadian pilots to fly its helicopters. They deliver interminable emotional speeches to which, after three vodkas from two-litre bottles, nobody listens. The Canadians, who have just arrived, look on in bewilderment. They see our plates piled high with steak specially flown in from Saudi.

'Isn't there supposed to be a famine here? Aren't they starving in Somalia? They always used to be.' The Canadian looks round inquiringly, but nobody even tries to explain what has gone wrong here in the past few months. The old hands have had it with Somalia.

New peace missions are about to be approved by the Security Council and the privateer circus is preparing to move on. Butch will hear shortly whether it is to be Haiti then Bosnia for him, or the other way round. He is hoping for Bosnia first. Doesn't know where it is, but does know that the wages are good: 'More than here. The danger money is higher.'

For Bruce it's Rwanda. The first contracts for a UN mission are doing the rounds. Bruce is after a big order for water pumps, to be installed in camps for Hutu refugees. Some of his colleagues are heading for Cuba: they've heard that the catering arrangements for Haitian boat refugees at the American base-turned-refugee camp at Guantánamo Bay are going to be privatized. The cheapest bidder will win the right to sell three meals a day for 40,000 refugees. And that number is rising by the hour, so the rumours will have us believe.

It could also be interesting to drop in on Washington, where Haiti's President Aristide is preparing to return in the wake of an American invasion. He is recruiting private bodyguards to take home with him.

I dance wild polkas with drunken Russians, between the tables and round behind the fridge, until deep in the night. The remains of our extravagant meal end up in the garbage. There would be more than enough to feed the refugees outside the gates. But nobody would dream of taking it out to them.

★

I leave Continue Hope to its own devices and head for Operation Support Democracy in Haiti.

The half past ten Hercules lifts off, bound for Mombasa. The sea below us is crystal clear. During my stay on the base I've never dared so much as to stick my toe in it. I soon learned the truth about those big fish I'd seen from the plane on the way in. The city's camel abattoir used to dump its waste in the sea at precisely the point where Port Base now stands. The sharks are still gathering there and have exchanged their previous scraps of camel for swimming blue helmets. Shark nets have been unable to prevent the occasional limb being gnawed.

On the cinema seat next to me in the hold sits Freddy, of the US 10th Mountain Division. He is one of the very last American soldiers left in Somalia and his turn for R&R has come up just before his evacuation.

'Sure I'm glad this operation is ending. At least for us. But the fun won't last long. It looks like the 10th Mountain are going to Bosnia, and maybe first an invasion of Haiti. Drives you crazy, a guy like Clinton, who lets himself get dragged into every piece of shit that comes his way. Know what I'd like? That all the Haitians, Somalis, Serbs, Tutsis, Hutsis and God knows where else we'll be sent, would go and sort out their own problems and that Clinton would just learn to say No for once.'

'Kill 'em All. Let God sort 'em out,' it says on the peak of his baseball cap.

## *VIII*

**American troops leave Somalia**

Mogadishu, 4 March 1994 – The final American troops left Somalia today, where they had been serving under the umbrella of the United Nations peacekeeping operation. 'We are proud of what we have done. We know we have kept hundreds of thousands of Somalis alive,' said General Thomas Montgomery, commander of the last American unit.

The Americans were waved out by Egyptian soldiers.                                                    (Reuters)

## 2. Haiti, Rwanda, Bosnia, Somalia and Thirteen Other Disaster Zones: Tailback in the Security Council

### American ambivalence

Washington, 18 January 1995 – The United States is deeply ambivalent over whether it wants a strong and effective United Nations. Americans would prefer unilateral solutions, but know that they cannot afford them. (*Washington Post*)

### UN troops take over operation from the US Army

New York, 20 January 1995 – The Security Council have given Boutros-Ghali the task of mobilizing 6,000 blue helmets for a peace mission in Haiti. The blue helmets are to take over the positions held by the US invasion force, which forced the military regime in Haiti to step down in Operation Restore Democracy. 'This decision of the Security Council is an outstanding example of the way in which the UN can co-operate with an intervention force,' explained the US Ambassador to the UN, Madeleine Albright. 'America can now share the burden of Haiti.' (UPI)

**UN bill for Haiti**

New York, 26 January 1995 – The 7,350 man
strong UN mission Uphold Democracy, which
will take over the work of the American army in
Haiti, will cost more than $178 million in the
first six months. This figure will cover 6,000 blue
helmets, 900 policemen, 227 civilian personnel,
193 local staff and 29 UN volunteers. The job
of Operation Uphold Democracy is to guarantee
security, set up a new police force and reform the
army.                                        (Reuters)

*I*

The costs facing American taxpayers for military intervention
in Haiti were initially far too high for US congressmen to
stomach. Haiti had by that time been boycotted by all its
trading partners for three years. A country that had always
been poverty-stricken was now completely bankrupt.

All the arguments against embarking on Clinton's invasion
of Haiti, code-named Operation Restore Democracy, had
been reviewed at length before the operation began: 'After
three years being economically drained, Haiti has become a
desert. Once we get in there, we'll never get out,' warned
one congressman.

'An invasion to restore democracy? Which has never existed
in Haiti!' was another astonished reaction.

'It will become a second Somalia. Every precondition for a
democracy is absent. No political parties, no professional
media, no trade unions.'

'No sign of any structure, either political or social, which
could carry anything that, in the far distant future, might

resemble a democracy. How would you knock one up, just like that? It would take years and cost a fortune.'

'There is no judicial system and no police force. There is absolutely nothing left in Haiti.'

'Potentially catastrophic.'

'Don't do it, Mr President, don't do it,' was the appeal of the Republican Chairman of the Senate Foreign Affairs Committee, Jesse Helms. But democracy had to be restored to solve an unnerving refugee problem. Clinton finally managed to win over Congress over by treating them to an explanation of his post-Somalia foreign policy. Which duly ensured that Haiti would indeed become a second Somalia, with both the American 'triumph' and the UN 'fiasco' repeated. 'If we start after breakfast, we'll be finished by lunchtime,' was the Pentagon's prediction for the conquest of Haiti. A guaranteed success and cheap into the bargain. Because in Haiti, as in Somalia, America would cover only the costs of the first part of the operation. The second part, Uphold Democracy, which was supposed to make a real country of Haiti, would be palmed off on the UN. And if the UN should fail? No problem. The UN will simply get the blame, as it did in Somalia. It should have said No.

So what can the UN do to protect itself over Haiti, when it has to send blue helmets out on a mission that has failed before it has begun? Answer: nothing. The UN cannot refuse to go: it receives an order to mobilize blue helmets and blue helmets are what it tries to mobilize. Yet here again it will find itself stranded in the midst of humanitarian chaos, charged with a fine-sounding assignment, coined by the Member States, that turns out to be quite unachievable. To uphold democracy in a bankrupt country where democracy has never existed. Go on, boys. Just do your best.

But as a desperate aid worker in Haiti once told me, 'The Haitian treasury is completely empty. In the three years of economic embargo we have barely managed to keep the Haitians alive. To make anything of this mess you'd need hundreds of millions of dollars every year, for years to come.' This vast sum would have to come from foreign investors. The very least such people would want to see before they would even consider, just possibly, coming to Haiti would be the rough outlines of a proper country. And for the metamorphosis of this economic wilderness into a democracy attractive enough for investors, a small peacekeeping force would be given . . . one year. Their inevitable failure would also have to be achieved on the cheap: when the resolution for Operation Uphold Democracy was adopted in the Security Council, only one of the 185 Member States did not owe money to the UN. Micronesia. With a micro contribution.

### UN obliged to borrow money from poor countries

Suva, 4 May 1995 – UN Secretary-General Boutros Boutros-Ghali said it was scandalous that the UN was effectively borrowing money from developing nations because rich countries had not paid their UN dues. On a three-day visit to Fiji, Boutros-Ghali said the United Nations owed Fiji almost $3 million for its contribution to peace-keeping operations in the Middle East and Africa. 'As long as the Member States don't pay up, they are effectively borrowing the money from your country, and without any interest.'        (Reuters)

## II

'The Organization is based on the principle of the sovereign equality of all nations' (Chapter 2.1 of the UN Charter). Which means: all nations are free to do and not do what they want within their own borders. The UN does not meddle in *coups d'état*. *Coups d'état*, however bloody, are internal affairs.

> **Bloody *coup d'état* in Haiti**
> Port-au-Prince, 30 September 1991 – Dozens were killed during a bloody coup in Haiti, in which the democratically elected president, Jean-Bertrand Aristide, was arrested by mutinous forces under the command of General Raoul Cédras. Hundreds of people were wounded. The French and American ambassadors, who hurried to Aristide's aid, have put pressure on the army not to murder the deposed president, but to allow him to leave the country. The Venezuelan president Perez has sent a plane to Haiti to collect him.　　　(AP, Reuters)

The United States, on the other hand, is allowed to meddle in Haiti's internal affairs. President Bush reacted to events in Port-au-Prince in resolute tones: 'When a democracy is menaced by the military, potentially dangerous shock waves run through this part of the world. We must make it clear to everyone that such misconduct has a terrible price. Until Aristide is restored to his position we will therefore ensure that the guilty parties are isolated from the rest of the world.'

The Organization of American States (OAS), representing all the countries of North and South America, promptly proclaimed a boycott against the coup leaders, which was then implemented by the US. Ninety-eight per cent of Haiti's imports come from OAS countries, mostly from the US. But Haitian regimes had never earned serious money via the official channels anyway. Thanks to the embargo the coup leaders made fortunes, partly from smuggling petrol and partly from the black market in food and medicines, the only products outside the embargo. It was thus not the junta, but the hungry who were driven out of Haiti. In the months following the coup, thousands of boat refugees were intercepted at sea by the United States Coastguard. The destitute bot pippel (the American phrase 'boat people', as pronounced in Haiti) were heading for Florida, some 900 kilometres north-east.

The junta, meanwhile, intensified their rule of terror. CNN was on the scene and put out pictures of victims, hacked beyond recognition by machetes. Whereupon the Democratic supporters of America's new President Clinton leapt indignantly to their feet and condemned their man's boat people policy as inhumane and immoral. He was sending refugees back into the clutches of murderers, just like Bush before him.

Clinton caved in: Haitians were given the right to apply for asylum. The American naval base at Guantánamo Bay on Cuba, a relative stone's throw from Haiti, was set up as a refugee camp. Intercepted boat people who qualified for political asylum could travel on to America. The rest could live in tents until the regime had stepped down and it was safe to return to Haiti.

The new policy was a disaster. The Coastguard were soon picking 3,000 refugees out of the sea every day. In Guantánamo Bay there was soon no room left for so much as a toddler and cruise ships had to be rented, into which new refugees could be stowed.

Meanwhile in New York, the Security Council was also a

hive of activity. The French were demanding blue helmets for Rwanda:

> 23 March 1993 – Between six and seven hundred thousand Rwandans are fleeing from a fresh outbreak of war between Hutus and Tutsis. Aid agencies are working at full stretch to prevent major epidemics. France has rushed to the aid of its old ally, the Rwandan Hutu government. A total of 900 French soldiers are defending the capital against an advance by Tutsi rebels. France wants 2,000 United Nations troops to come and relieve its forces.                                        (*Trouw*)

And the Americans were demanding 30,000 blue helmets for their project in Somalia.

### Somalia: mission half accomplished
Washington, 17 May 1993 – To the US military, their job in Somalia is finished. The hand-over to the UN officially began on May 1 when Secretary-General Boutros-Ghali started paying the bills.
                                        (*Time Magazine*)

The UN mission in Rwanda was barely on track when the UN mission in Somalia came off the rails, less than six months after it had begun. When eighteen American soldiers were killed in Mogadishu, the US cancelled all co-operation with the UN mission immediately and withdrew its forces from Somalia.

> New York, 18 October 1993 – [Boutros-Ghali] listened with astonishment to Clinton's speech to

the UN, in which the American President reproached the UN for repeatedly shouldering tasks that were too heavy for it. 'The UN should learn to say No,' said Clinton. (*International Herald Tribune*)

The UN cannot say No to blue helmets for Somalia and Rwanda, any more than to blue helmets for Bosnia, Palestine, Kashmir, Cyprus, the Golan Heights, Lebanon, Iraq, Kuwait, Angola, El Salvador, Western Sahara, Mozambique, Georgia and Liberia. A total of 17,000 UN soldiers were already deployed over sixteen different missions. Two days after Clinton advised the UN to say No, on 20 October 1993, the US cheerfully requested that a UN fleet of ships be despatched to help surround Haiti. No longer involved in Continue Hope in Somalia, the Americans now wanted an Operation Support Democracy in Haiti, demanding in the Security Council that the UN contribute to solving the problems associated with the regime in Haiti. According to them, there were now so many Haitian refugees drifting about on the Caribbean that destabilization was threatening the whole region. Pointing to the Security Council's obligation to guarantee international peace and security, America insisted that all UN Member States should join the OAS boycott of Haiti and that ships be provided to enforce it.

The Security Council agreed. Sea routes to and from Haiti were henceforth to be cut by a multi-national UN fleet. All sea traffic, notably all rotting sailing boats, improvised rafts and bathtubs full of bot pippel, was to be confined to Haitian coastal waters. Refugees who had already made it to Guantánamo Bay could stay there, but any new bot pippel were to be intercepted and sent home.

After the imposition of Operation Support Democracy, anyone who still tried to escape from the economic starvation of

Haiti simply hadn't a chance. Haiti became a prison in which her people were locked up with their junta and no food.

Support Democracy failed. The Haitian regime remained coolly in place and went on with its smuggling.

That same spring, UN operations elsewhere in the world were proving, if possible, even less successful:

### American troops leave Somalia

Mogadishu, 4 March 1994 – The final American troops left Somalia today, where they had been serving under the umbrella of the United Nations peace-keeping operation. 'We are proud of what we have done. We know we have kept hundreds of thousands of Somalis alive,' said General Thomas Montgomery, commander of the last American unit.

The Americans were waved out by Egyptian soldiers. (Reuters)

### Belgium pulls its troops out of Rwanda

Kigali, 14 April 1994 – 'We will not stay under any conditions.' With these words the Belgian Foreign Minister Willy Claes put an axe to the roots of the UN mission in Rwanda, where the civil war has flared up again in spite of the peace accord. Claes has informed Boutros-Ghali that Brussels wishes to withdraw from the UN force. Ten Belgian blue helmets have been violently killed.

'The mission has no point any more. Blue helmets have not been able to prevent more than 20,000 people being killed in a few days. And the situation is getting ever more chaotic,' said an emotional Claes.

The 400 or so Belgian blue helmets formed the linchpin of the 2,500-strong UN Force. Boutros-Ghali has asked the Security Council to consider simply ending the mission in Rwanda.

(Reuters, AFP)

## Bosnia: painful comedown for Boutros-Ghali

20 April 1994 – The UN is having to look on powerless as the Serbs violate Gorazde. For some time the Serbs have been ignoring appeals by the Security Council. Boutros-Ghali is being forced to consider whether the peacekeeping force in Bosnia is serving any purpose. It has certainly helped the population get through two winters and has prevented famine, but blue helmets have had no influence at all on the military course of the war.

(*Financieel Dagblad*)

## The UN bogged down at fifty

When he took office in 1991, UN Secretary-General Boutros Boutros-Ghali promised comprehensive reform. He moved quickly to eliminate one-third of the high-level posts and consolidate overlapping offices. But then he became distracted. 'I don't think managerial issues are his favorite issues,' said U.S. Ambassador Madeleine Albright. 'He had some very good ideas at the beginning but he became bogged down. I think he thought it would be easier . . .' The Secretary-General is no longer convinced that trimming is what the United Nations needs . . . 'The problem is to add new personnel because of the new demands.

We are overloaded with demands.'

(*Washington Post*, 2 January 1995)

But the tailback in the Security Council would only get longer . . .

## III

*Haiti, April 1994*

Haiti is the shabby end of the island of Hispaniola, which she shares with the Dominican Republic. In the past it used to seem like a giant had been employed to lift up the island from the Dominican end and shake it, so that all the garbage would tumble down to the Haitian end. The rotting piles in Haitian streets were often more than head height. But now the garbage is finished. Because of the embargo, the piles are getting smaller and smaller. People and animals have eaten the remains and nobody has new garbage to throw away. The children's eyes follow their mothers as they scour the streets from side to side looking for anything edible.

But my fried chicken is served à la Créole. The chewed bones go over the wall on to the pavement. When I see the women fighting over them with stray dogs, the contents of my stomach nearly follow them. I have landed up back in Haiti, one of my old stamping grounds, in the middle of the UN's Operation Restore Democracy.

**America does not rule out violence against Haiti**
Washington, 30 April 1994 – The United States is considering 'all options', including the possible use of force to oust the military regime in Haiti,

administration officials said Saturday. Any military
action could involve units from the 82nd Airborne Division and the US Special Operations
Command.                                        (Reuters)

It is nine o'clock in the morning and high time for me to
report to the American Embassy in Port-au-Prince for the
daily press conference, given by spokesman Stanley Schrager.
'Yes, off you go, off to see beautiful Stanley. Just write down
the threats. Tell him that God will deal with him at the
gates of Heaven.' The cackling laugh of Annette Ahmad, my
hotelière, pursues me out into the street. I don't find a taxi.
The embargo has seriously thinned out the taxi fleet in Haiti.
I walk the 3 kilometres through the city. After three years of
economic strangulation, a resignation bordering on apathy
prevails. Due to the high price of smuggled petrol, it is no
longer maniacs on taptap-buses who are the main danger, but
people crossing the road. They wander around numbly and
react late to the blast of a horn. Whole families wait out the
day under the trees in front of the Presidential Palace, passive,
their babies beside them on the paving stones. I note that any
invader would simply be able to walk into the Palace: one of
the wrought-iron gates hangs permanently open, twisted on
the hinge. But for the time being the battle with Clinton is being
fought out with graffiti and it's still not clear who will win the
nomination for 'Most Mentioned', Clinton or the Brazilian
footballer Romario, either '*Viv!*' or '*A bas!*'

A mother washes her three toddlers in the thick ooze which
flows slowly through an open drain. Journalists step over the
little family: we are right outside the office of USIS, the United
States Information Service. Since the Americans decided to
communicate their Haiti policy to the foreign press from this
very office, correspondents have dubbed it the 'Beacon of

Democracy'. The message from 'the beacon' is always the same: democracy will prevail in Haiti, whatever the cost.

'Beautiful Stanley' has a head full of dents and creases and he chews his fingers to bloody stumps, even while taking questions. Since Washington has required him to persuade the press that Clinton really means it when he talks about military intervention, he has also developed a nervous tic: every few seconds he has to sniff up and swallow a mouthful of phlegm. An extremely objectionable habit, whose sound is greatly magnified by the audio-visual equipment upon which he relies.

The room contains only fourteen journalists: most of the others have left Haiti and gone to the war in Rwanda. Television lights flicker on and the buttons of cassette recorders are pressed as Stanley ascends the kidney-shaped podium.

'The embargo is becoming more and more effective,' he begins. 'Food prices have at least trebled. Social unrest will soon be breaking out and that is the last thing the junta needs.' After this announcement, he looks round the room brightly.

'When's the invasion, Stan?' somebody calls.

'As soon as it's needed,' answers Schrager and smiles.

The *Washington Post* doodles stick men in an otherwise empty notebook. Haiti is bound for page six, bottom right. The world's press is going to lead on Rwanda.

### 'All Tutsis in Rwanda murdered'

Ngara, 3 May 1994 – A quarter of a million Rwandan refugees have crossed the border within twenty-four hours. The exodus is so overwhelming that aid workers with the UN refugee organization UNHCR can only look on in dismay. The Rwandans are fleeing from the war between the Hutu government army and Tutsi rebels. Accord-

ing to four Belgian monks, just evacuated, there
are no more Tutsis left alive in Rwanda.

The UN has withdrawn all but 450 of its peacekeeping force in Rwanda.

(*de Volkskrant*, Reuters)

After question time with Stanley I take breakfast at the Hotel
Oloffson. This haven for foreign journalists is indispensable in
a country where the local media go along with the regime's
lies and foreign papers fall under the embargo. At the Oloffson
you still hear something sometimes. And on the breakfast
tables you can find faxes from home desks, briefing correspondents on what the competition is reporting from Haiti.
Not much at the moment, it seems, compared with all the
news from Rwanda.

'*Chérie!* I just knew you would come.' Aubelin Jolicoeur,
society columnist for the Haitian paper *Le Nouvelliste*, greets
me effusively on the veranda. He rubs his fragile, seventy-year-
old body against my bosom and coos: 'Have you come to save
your dear little Aubelin from the big bad Americans?'

'Frightened of an invasion, Aubelin?' I ask, buttering my
toast.

'Aubelin Jolicoeur is not frightened of anything, darling. I
am a carefree butterfly, placed here on earth to be happy
and beautiful,' he says, and nibbles on a crust of bread and
marmalade. 'We were discussing it only yesterday, *le général et
moi-même*. Raoul Cédras has no plans to resign. *Au contraire* –
he is going to hold presidential elections and make sure that
he wins. Then he will be a democratically elected president,
just like Aristide. Gives you what you want and saves us from
your interference.'

Jolicoeur is the Nigel Dempster of Haiti. He knows everyone who matters and they know him. Anywhere local or foreign VIPs gather, Aubelin will be there. In Haiti's golden years, when the country could still be sold as a holiday destination, he virtually filled every edition of *Le Nouvelliste* on his own. He would lie in wait for cruise ships carrying VIPs at the harbour, pursue the ladies and gentlemen to banquets and soirées in full evening dress, fill the newspaper's columns with their adventures and romances in Haiti and wave them goodbye after their holidays. He still goes through life in dress clothes – 'You will not find me dead without a breast-pocket handkerchief' – but no VIPs come to Haiti these days, except as diplomats, in which case they are forbidden to hobnob with the local elite: representatives of UN Member States no longer officially talk to supporters of the regime.

Calling them names is allowed, however. On the club circuit, diplomats have introduced the term 'MRE' to describe the local elite. In Somalia this meant 'Meals Ready to Eat' for GIs. In Haiti it means 'Morally Repugnant Elite'. *Les riches (nouveaux* or otherwise), to whom this phrase applies, feel deeply insulted, but the fact remains that 90 per cent of all incoming wealth disappears into the pockets of 10 per cent of the population. The elite simply want to spend it all on themselves. The poor, for all they care, can quite literally drop dead.

Aubelin wipes away an imaginary breadcrumb from the corner of his mouth with a spotless white handkerchief. 'I will put you in the paper, *chérie*,' he promises. Then, swinging his gold-handled cane over a narrow shoulder, he skips down the stairs to the garden and disappears into the untrimmed shrubbery.

Now and then a hoarded supply of petrol explodes in someone's shed or back garden. My first reaction is always to think that the invasion has begun.

Petrol stations, closed for three years now, may be covered with thick layers of dust but they are not abandoned. As long as there's a roof, the homeless are sitting under it. Several families are camping under the canopy of the Shell station on Boulevard la Saline, down by the harbour. Since the embargo the Boulevard, with its long lines of people hawking smuggled petrol in jerry cans and plastic lemonade bottles, has become known as Kuwait City. The border with the Dominican Republic is officially closed, but in practice it leaks like a sieve: petrol and diesel are expensive (half a day's wage for a litre) but there is enough and some to spare. The hawkers, slipping on the greasy road surface, beckon to passing cars with funnels made from cans of American cooking oil. They thump and kick each other to be first to grab hold of our petrol cap. The winner is in such a hurry to pour his gallon into the tank that I am spattered with petrol.

The markets are empty because farm produce is no longer transported. Smuggled petrol is too dear for farmers. But harvests were already falling because the export of fertilizer to Haiti was banned. And anyway, the farmers don't have enough money left to buy seed.

The urban population, without income, hangs around on the street. Many of them used to have jobs assembling base-balls, electrical goods and clothing. Since the international embargo on goods 'Made in Haiti', factory owners have been gradually closing their gates. They have left for other Latin American countries, firmly resolved never to return.

People have become homeless because they now have to buy food with the money intended for rent. They borrow and pawn until everything has gone. Then they get hungry and then they get sick. In schools, hospitals, churches and clinics throughout the country, aid agencies are distributing food supplements. Since the embargo came into force, they have seen their clientele rise from 350,000 to 1.7 million – almost one in four Haitians. Meanwhile, half the children in Haiti are malnourished, in Port-au-Prince up to two-thirds. Every day starving children are abandoned on the steps of churches and hospitals. 'When did you last eat?' is often my question to Haitians. 'A few days ago,' is usually the vague answer.

In the harbour it stinks of rotting food. Containers packed with consignments of food aid are standing on the quayside: food and medicines do not fall under the embargo. Some of them have been there for months. I find a *gardien* mooching about and ask him what's going on. He grins broadly. 'In that one there are sacks of oatmeal and further up you've got beans. The containers only get opened if the senders officially apply to General Cédras.' A dark strategy to secure a semblance of recognition for the boycotted regime. New consignments seldom arrive.

On the street you trip over the beggars, while the prisons are full of people who saw no other way to survive but to steal. A fourteen-year-old apple thief was arrested in one village yesterday. The local military commander, who calls himself Saddam Hussein and behaves accordingly, cut off the ear of the fruit robber and said: 'If you're hungry, eat this.' Then he carved his initials in the boy's buttocks and beat him with a stick, 150 strokes.

### Boutros-Ghali disappointed in embargo

New York, 4 May 1994 – The UN Secretary-General said today that the international community should back off and encourage Haitians to sort out their political future by themselves. Boutros Boutros-Ghali said the international community risks becoming involved in 'too heavy a task'. 'Given that negotiations have not brought

about any significant progress, it seems fitting
to recommend that a more specifically Haitian
solution should be found.'                          (AP)

But Clinton is not to be stopped. Democracy must and will
be restored, by violence if necessary.

Invasions are expensive. But they get a bit cheaper if you
can dispose of the booty soon after the conquest.

> **America recruits troops for UN force Haiti**
> Washington, 10 May 1994 – The US is trying to
> persuade Latin American countries to make troops
> available for an international peacekeeping force in
> Haiti. Their task would be to oversee the restor-
> ation of the Aristide government after a US
> invasion. Secretary of State Warren Christopher
> again warned that Haiti 'must pay the price' if it
> continued to refuse to agree to the return of Aris-
> tide. Madeleine Albright, US Ambassador to the
> UN, yesterday repeated that America is not ruling
> out a military intervention.              (AP, Reuters)

At Pétionville, the millionaire suburb high in the hills above
Port-au-Prince, I am discovering how pleasant it is to play
tennis with the morally repugnant elite. Until the name Aristide is dropped into the conversation. Then steam rises from
ears and foam issues from the corners of mouths.

'Necrophiliac!' 'Hitler and Stalin rolled into one!' 'A
dangerous lunatic!', 'Cannibal!', 'Ayatollah!' – the harvest of
five minutes' talk on the gravel court of the Pétionville Tennis
Club. I had raised the subject by asking what people thought
of the American plan to restore democracy by bringing back
Aristide. The MREs end the interview by stamping away to

the dressing rooms. It will take a long time for members to forgive my host Louis (from the security department of the French Embassy) for introducing me as a guest.

'They are certainly feeling the strain,' I say, as doors slam behind furious backs.

'Not really,' says Louis, inspecting the strings of his racket. 'What you just saw was mortal terror. America is linking the concept "democracy" to the person Aristide. But it is the phenomenon itself that terrifies the elite. Democracy stands for *liberté, égalité et fraternité* and so on. Housemaids with as much right to a say as their employers. There is nothing more scary to an MRE.'

Louis plays tennis with the elite three times a week and after four years as a member can describe the attitude in Haitian tennis clubs like nobody else: 'They're the same as the Afrikaners. They were convinced that Apartheid was God's intention and that democracy can lead to nothing but chaos and death. The MREs were born as masters over slaves. That's the way it was before the elections that put Aristide in the Presidential Palace, that's how it has remained since, in spite of the elections, and that's how it must remain, because that's how it should be.'

The rich 10 per cent of the population have never seen the filthy slums on either side of the harbour where the other 90 per cent live, let alone smelled them. Louis sums up the attitude of his tennis partners as follows: 'Let them do what they like in the nigger huts *là-bas*, just as long as we aren't bothered by it.' And so the MREs put up virtually no resistance when, under pressure from the Americans, elections were held in 1991. They just didn't take part. 'Let the Americans do what they like, just as long as we aren't bothered by it,' was their consistent line once again.

The fact that elections were held, more or less honestly, for the first time in the 200 years of Haitian history did not mean that the country suddenly became a democracy. Elections are the exception in Haiti, coups the rule.

Only the poor voted, thus their favourite, the slum priest Aristide, emerged as the winner. The people found this American idea of democracy tremendous, until they discovered that from now on a new president would have to be chosen every few years. Democracy immediately became slightly less interesting. Unfair even. They thought they had elected Aristide for life. All Haitian presidents have more or less intended to stay president for life, so why not the People's President?

There have been more than a hundred transfers of power in Haiti's 200-year history; most presidencies, life-long or not, have come to a premature end via coups. The coup against Aristide came within seven months.

'The devil . . .' begins Mike. He falters. He can't bring himself to utter Aristide's name. 'The devil . . . swans around Washington with a diamond-encrusted Rolex on his wrist. Did you know that?' Mike is the American owner of three businesses closed down by the embargo.

A few drams later and he can't come up with the Christian name of that other son-of-a-bitch, 'Goddamn Perry Clinton or whatever his name is', who is plotting with Amnesty International and Boutros Boutros-Ghali 'to bring a maniac back to Haiti'.

'A hundred empty hotel rooms, two empty swimming pools and an empty casino,' Mike raves on. 'My factory, blue jeans for the American market? Closed. I've already had to lay off several hundred Haitians. All the fault of those dangerous madmen in New York and Washington with their Operation Support Democracy.

'But we're not going to die of hunger,' says Mike. 'Not yet. There's still food to buy in our shops. We start up our generators when the rest of the city is without lights. But more and more Haitians have less and less money to buy food with. Soon they'll be murdering me for what's in my fridge. But I've decided to shoot as many as I can before they get me. Survival of the fittest, man.' He has lived here long enough to make a gesture I have seen many Haitians use. It is as if they are knocking something dirty from their hands. '*Pa fot mwen*', is what it means. Not my fault.

I start to take a notebook from my bag and Mike's rott-weilers, sniffing at my ankles, growl and bare their teeth. Their master laughs. 'Don't worry,' he says. 'They never bite *blancs*.'

A pile of street children are asleep under pieces of plastic, arms and legs protruding from all sides. They lie on top of each other, across each other and in each other's arms. This morning I have risen at half past three to ring through to a radio station in Hilversum. Haiti is six hours behind the Netherlands. The phone in the Prestige, where I stay, is broken again and the Ahmad family, owners of this once luxurious hotel, are not planning to get it repaired. I walk to the Hotel Oloffson.

Bats skim through the dark lobby. Apart from them, I am alone. So, after fiddling with the wires and plugs, I operate the switchboard myself.

Radio 1 News has dropped Haiti for today and replaced it with cholera in the refugee camps for Rwandans in Zaire. Much more interesting. But as I hang up on Hilversum, the switchboard lights flicker again: Goma, Zaire, on the line.

'Hello! This is Vera . . . (crackle) . . . Calling from Goma . . . (whistle) . . . James there, please?'

I insert a plug: 'Which James?'

'. . . you see James, tell him we're all in Goma. Tell him to come too. Big story here . . . (whistle) . . . all dead.'

It looks as if James is already on his way. He is not among the handful of journalists who appear for breakfast. All the interesting faxes must be going to Goma too: there's not one about us in Haiti this morning. We seem to be bucking the trend.

Yesterday France was demanding that recently evacuated blue helmets should immediately return to save the last surviving Rwandans. Today the Americans are doing their best to get the French proposal dismissed as 'impossible'.

### America calls UN plan for Rwanda 'over-ambitious'

New York, 13 May 1994 – The US has criticized a new French plan to send 5,500 UN soldiers into the heart of the Rwandan civil war, arguing that it is more than the organization can handle. UN troops would not be allowed to use force to bring an end to the genocide in Rwanda, which has already cost an estimated 200,000 lives.

*(New York Times)*

Whoopi Goldberg stars in tonight's film at the Rex Cinema on the Champs de Mars. If there is any electricity. But between six and eight in the morning people queue at the box office for political asylum. Complaints have reached Clinton from the grass roots of the Democratic Party that Haitians with a right to asylum have been left stranded by the UN marine cordon. People whose lives are at risk in Haiti ought to be offered a way out. There are on average a hundred people a day in the queue. They get a form to fill in and, a few weeks later, a letter from Washington rejecting their application.

For the asylum seekers it is, as always, all about *gran gou*, big hunger. That's the literal translation at least. But if someone says he has *gran gou*, he really means that his whole life is a vale of tears.

A man at the front of the queue recounts how his boat trip to Miami came to grief in the previous week. 'In a sailing boat, my eleven-year-old son, myself and twenty-four others.' He had packed a sack of rice, a jar of peanut butter and a clean pair of trousers (without holes) for the trip. 'We had sailed for two days before we were picked up by an American ship. The soldiers asked why we wanted to go to Miami and I explained that I was a carpenter, with a wife and four children, and that I can't find any more customers and can't afford to buy food. *Gran gou*.'

The Americans had hoisted the refugees aboard their ship and given them food and water, but they were very unfriendly. 'Angry,' says the man. 'They said that there were too many people like us and that we were driving them crazy. They did not take us to Guantánamo Bay, but straight back to Port-au-Prince. But I still have *gran gou*, and I want to tell that to the Americans at the cinema. Maybe these ones will understand.'

The man doesn't dare to risk another sea crossing. 'I sold my radio, my table and my bed to be able to buy the tickets for the trip and we could easily have sunk on the way. The captain had no charts and no compass and didn't know exactly where Miami was. The boat was overloaded. Sometimes these captains push you overboard if their boat looks like capsizing.'

A thin American lady, a schoolteacher type with severe spectacles and a blue pleated skirt, checks to see if everyone in the queue has the requisite passport photos with them, black and white in duplicate. She reprimands those who don't fit the bill. To an old man with bare feet she says, 'Didn't we reject you last week?'

The man nods.

'So what are you doing here again?'

'Today worse than last week,' he says. '*Mwen gran gou.*'

In Amsterdam you get used to the clatter of trams. In Port–au–Prince to bursts of machine-gun fire. The regime's henchmen are on the loose again. After a night full of shooting, through which I comfortably sleep, I am woken by a loud bang outside the hotel gates, followed by screaming and crying.

'Two taptaps, collided at full speed,' pants Fritz, the receptionist at the Prestige. I don't go to look at the accident. If the onlookers see a *blanc*, a foreigner, they expect them to take over and perform miracles.

Fritz, puffing up and down, announces one dead and four injured. The injured won't make it, I reckon. The only operations still carried out take place in the MRE hospital in Pétionville. The people's Hôpital Général can no longer sterilize its instruments.

I wander from my room on to the veranda, order coffee and leaf through *Le Nouvelliste*. In the Security Council, America is lobbying the Russians to join them in voting against blue helmets for Rwanda:

### US and Russia against peacekeeping force for Rwanda

New York, 13 May 1994 – The chances of the UN sending a peacekeeping force to Rwanda seem slight. Yesterday the Russians followed America in turning down the French plan. The US Ambassador to the UN, Madeleine Albright, made clear that Washington had major objections to an intervention in the Rwandan bloodbath because of the costs and the risks involved.     (*Guardian*, AFP)

Rather than walking into a predictable fiasco in Rwanda, UN Member States should swoop down on Haiti. A UN peace mission in Haiti would be a lot safer and much cheaper. Or so American officials assure potential blue helmet providers. They are on a recruiting mission, during which they are loudly extolling Haiti as a destination. Pentagon spies have revealed that the Haitian army consists of 7,400 barely trained soldiers, of whom roughly half have a working rifle at their disposal. The Haitian navy has one ship with engines that go. Plus a few other boats that may float, but not convincingly enough to put to sea. There are also some helicopters that have been parked next to the runway for years. They look just as worn out as Haitian taptaps. You could not imagine a softer opponent for an international force than the army of the poorest country in the Western hemisphere, say the Americans.

### Haiti's army not seen as potent fighting force

Port-au-Prince, 17 May 1994 – The Haitian army has prepared its defences against a possible American invasion. A broken-down tank has been recently placed in the car park at the back of the Quartier Général, the Haitian military headquarters, while a WWII fieldgun has been set up in the bushes on the other side of the street. After soldiers had bolted the weapon together, various parts were still left in the cardboard packing. Two Haitian soldiers were asleep on park benches next to the box. 'This is pretty typical of the level of military resources in Haiti,' said a European defence expert. (*Los Angeles Times*)

American recruiters, seeking to enthuse potential supporters, claim to know that the Haitian military command is intending to adopt so-called 'evaporation tactics' in the event of an attack: i.e. their soldiers will take off their uniforms and go into hiding. The only real threat to anyone helping restore Haitian democracy will, they say, be the malaria mosquito.

But for the time being Haiti is no match for Rwanda in the Security Council.

### UN pledges blue helmets for Rwanda

New York, 18 May 1994 – After an extremely arduous debate, the UN Security Council has unanimously agreed to expand the UN peacekeeping mission in Rwanda to 5,500 men. The slowness of the decision-making process was caused by the Americans, who want to reduce the number of UN peacekeeping missions. According to Washington, the operation in Rwanda is surrounded by too many uncertainties and is thereby in conflict with President Clinton's new foreign policy. In Rwanda the Tutsi rebels have immediately warned that UN soldiers deployed between themselves and Hutu government-troops will be regarded as enemy units. The rebels also said that they would ignore the appeal for a cease-fire included in the resolution.          (Reuters)

The Prestige Hotel could pass as a rest home for geriatric supporters of the regime. The owner Moïse Ahmad is ninety-two, his wife Annette eighty-three. Their three permanent guests must be around the hundred mark. Every morning the old folks shuffle in careful procession over the slippery tiles of the hotel galleries, one hand on the walking stick, the other groping the wall for support.

The Ahmads are millionaires. Moïse Ahmad's father came to Haiti from Lebanon in 1881. He married a local girl and, like many Lebanese at the time, opened a grocery store. The trade is still controlled by Arab families.

Moïse has been a schoolmaster, electrician, mechanic and icemaker, but his big break came when he ran five banana boats back and forth to America during the Second World War. He used the profits to buy the Prestige Hotel, which stands next to the Presidential Palace on a piece of ground which is now worth a fortune. In spite of the worldwide ban on trade with Haiti and Haitians, an American businessman recently offered him $2 million for it. Moïse turned him down and has since complained constantly about poverty, in chorus with his retired son, middle-aged daughter and boorish 28-year-old grandson, Grégoire. 'We haven't got half a gourde left in our pockets because of that embargo of yours,' he whines, when I ask if one of them can change a fifty-gourde note.

All the Ahmads have flats at the back of the hotel and I never see any of them rise from their cane rocking chairs on the spacious veranda. They bask comfortably in their victim status.

'Of course we would like to be working and creating employment, but we can't, because, yes, you know, the embargo,' they say, triumphantly aggrieved. They have recently fired nearly all their hotel staff for lack of guests. 'What are the poor people of Haiti not having to suffer under your embargo! And what a mess those blue helmets of yours will soon have to clear up. Terrible!' All the lazily rocking Ahmads shake their heads. 'But yes, this Operation Support Democracy is apparently worth ruining everything for.' Grandson Grégoire lets his mouth hang open like a moron and then adds a squint. He is imitating a slum-dweller. 'Demacracie? Wot is dat?' He puts on an imbecile voice. Annette Ahmad finds it terribly funny. So I return to Beautiful Stanley at the Beacon of Democracy to be briefed on the arguments for an invasion, to be followed by a UN peacekeeping mission.

'*La journaliste ravissante hollandaise Linda Palmal* is also against an intervention,' I read in Aubelin's society column. True to his word, he has put me in *Le Nouvelliste*. I quickly stuff the paper down between two chairs. There are ten journalists left in the USIS room. The rest have all gone to Rwanda.

'The UN fleet has only had to save 200 boat people from drowning this week. The figure used to be 3,000 a day, you will remember. Operation Support Democracy is an enormous success,' says Stanley Schrager.

Reuters raises his finger: 'When's the invasion, Stan?'

'Soon,' replies Schrager. 'At least, if it's still necessary. The regime is tottering. Just wait until UN patrols have plugged the final holes in the border with the Dominican Republic.'

While three-quarters of the population cannot read or write, most of the children in Haiti have not been to school for three years. The schools are closed because people can't spare the admission fees, so there's no money to pay the teachers. The Haitian-American Institute is a language school in Port-au-Prince. Its principal, an American woman, looks exhausted. She is drinking too much. With an unsteady hand she lights up another Comme Il Faut cigarette.

'Twenty years ago I taught Haitian children an English vocabulary which would allow them to study medicine or law in the States. After the coup against Aristide I gave a crash course in slang. Just in case the boat made it to Florida and they were picked up by the immigration service. I taught them to say things like "Yo, motherfucker, you sayin' I ain't American just 'cause I's a nigger?" They still had some hope then. Now, with the blockade, they haven't got a chance. So the Institute is closed. No more students.'

We are dining in Pétionville, the only place in the country where, with a little effort, you can imagine you're not in Haiti. There are discotheques and stores where you can buy cordless telephones and computers. True, the supermarkets are smelling mouldier every day and they no longer sell fresh or frozen products. But the tinned fancy pink salmon and the Beaujolais Nouveau are still on the shelves. And they say that the few hundred square metres that make up this suburb of Port-au-Prince are now home to a few dozen more millionaires than before the embargo.

Eating within sight of the hungry Haitians who have climbed the hill from the slums *là-bas* is, once again, not a success. The dinner is nerve-racking. We order spaghetti. I don't know the restaurant's real name, but the journalists call it Cindy's Place, after the prostitute who invariably manages to find us here. She hangs around the gate to the terrace until she sees someone she knows, then minces over to him, pulls up a chair and joins the meal. Her mini-skirted, high-heeled friends in the street jump out in front of the kerb-crawling cars. They are little girls dressed up in women's clothes. More and more of them are working the same patch, which leads to screaming rows. Potential clients let them parade in front of the headlights before they start negotiating a price for what they have seen. Apart from the clamour of the hookers, we have to endure the screaming of street children, who are after the leftovers from our plates, and keep out the cacophony produced by a perambulating combo playing old Beatles numbers. We collect some money just to shut them up.

Is our perception distorted by vexation, or are there really more cripples stumbling round than before? Every few minutes we seem to see somebody passing by with deformed limbs.

'People no longer get their broken arms and legs reset and put in plaster. They can't afford it,' says Dr Frantz Large. He sits grimly behind a plate of French fries at the next table. 'I don't see any more patients at my surgery because people know that I'm going to prescribe medicines they can't pay for, even if they're in stock. The hospital is almost empty for the same reason: you can lie in a bed for free, but you have to find and pay for medicines and bandages yourself. We still have a few nurses who push beds into the dry whenever it rains. The roof leaks, of course. Six months ago three shiploads of medical aid arrived. Nobody knows what happened to it. If you guys go looking for it, you'll probably find it costing a fortune up here in the drugstores of Pétionville, or maybe in the Dominican Republic.' Dr Large laughs a tired and humourless laugh.

Today I want to visit Michel François. This sinister character led the coup against Aristide, after which he appointed himself Chief of Police. In Haiti this means the hated, military form of the profession. François is one of the military Band of Three whose resignation is being demanded by the USA. The other two are Raoul Cédras and Philippe Biamby, the army number two.

François has only agreed to an interview twice in his life, one of which was with the Dutch newspaper *NRC Handelsblad*. But although his name is on everyone's lips, you get the impression that he doesn't really exist. He rules like a phantom. Nobody knows precisely what he thinks or even what he looks like. A photographer with the Associated Press has earned a basic income for years from the only photo of the Chief of Police that appears in the press archives. It shows François in profile, with his helmet on his knees. A podgy black man, at that moment engaged in an apparently amusing conversation with General Cédras. François is smiling. Cruelly, I imagine.

His headquarters is painted mustard yellow, the colour of the army. On the floor behind the desk in the hall sit eight men, chained together, facing the wall. Their heads are hanging. One if them is crying. '*Ils sont des amis*,' says the duty sergeant, laughing. And François, as always, is unavailable.

François provides his followers with a pistol, the title 'attaché', and a licence to rob and intimidate. The attachés are held to be responsible for the daily murders in the slums. Some time ago CNN, who can never get hold of François either, discovered a second man behind the attachés: Emmanuel Constant. Toto to his admirers.

'We belong to the FRAPH, the Front for Progress and Democracy, the voice of the people,' Toto duly announced, in an interview broadcast live throughout the world. Thus the civil arm of Michel François's terror regime acquired the status of a political party on the international stage. The members of FRAPH like to parade through the street with machine guns and the pistols that François has given them. FRAPH is known as the 'Rent-a-Mob Company', a kind of job agency for rioters and vandals. '*Quand on est du FRAPH, on frappe*': 'FRAPH' sounds very like the French *frapper* – to hit – which is exactly what its members do. They lash out at anything they don't fancy.

Toto Constant claims to have several hundred thousand followers: 'If not millions, at least. You know how difficult it is to arrive at figures in Haiti.' If you want to speak to the man himself, you have to go to his local bar, which functions as his office. La Normandie is close to the Palace, wedged between a travel agency (which has had no customers for years) and an undertakers (which has had far too many). Until very recently, you could find Toto here from early in the morning until late at night, benignly rocking on a kitchen chair reserved for him by the owner, a glass of rum before him. Soldiers were often there too, drinking with Toto. You could see him looking out through the café railings, with evident satisfaction, to the members of his fan club assembled on the pavement: an army of unemployed down-and-outs, waiting. Sometimes Toto was planning a demonstration, and on those days he'd hand out rum and maybe some loose change.

These days the press has to make do without him: Toto has moved on from rum to crack and is not always in any condition to be able to find La Normandie. Rumour has it that he's smuggled eighty-six Bingo games clean through the UN blockade from Miami, so his followers are still waiting. The men, boys and occasional women hang around, glaring at passers-by, inspecting the exhausts of each other's mopeds, daubing 'Viv Toto!' on walls and cursing Aristide when a journalist turns up for an interview.

'*Aristide cannibal!*' yell a few FRAPHers as I walk up. They put on their moped helmets and look tough.

'Where is Toto?' I ask.

'In a meeting,' someone shouts angrily.

'Is there another leader around?' I don't have a name to hand – Toto's deputies change from day to day, just like his hangers-on.

'I kill you, dirty American,' screams someone else.

'No, don't kill her. She can interview me,' says a heavy on a moped with coloured ribbons sprouting from the handgrips.

'Kill her!' shrieks a fat woman in a mini-skirt.

'Where is Michel François?' I try again, but when somebody

with a pistol starts to get involved, I walk away. I don't really need to hear the FRAPH view of Operation Support Democracy anyway.

The UN estimates that 45,000 refugees have fled from Haiti since the coup. Support Democracy is still not getting anywhere and saving the Rwandans doesn't seem to be working either. You might almost be tempted to blame the UN:

> ### Boutros admits UN failing Rwanda
> New York, 26 May 1994 – Boutros-Ghali yesterday admitted that the UN has not succeeded in finding the extra soldiers needed to bring the UN mission in Rwanda up to 5,500 men. 'I have failed,' said Boutros-Ghali. 'It is a scandal. I am the first to say it and I am ready to repeat it.' He has, he says, 'implored' the international community to make troops available.                    (*NRC Handelsblad*, AP)

Today *Le Nouvelliste* reports that the death toll in Rwanda has now reached a million.

'Excuse me. I have one dead body for you.'

I am taking coffee with John, a press bureau photographer, at the Oloffson.

'Oh yeah? What kind of body?' he asks from behind his *Nouvelliste*.

'Man. Young. Hands tied behind his back. Machete wounds in his face,' replies the body guide.

'What do you want for him?' inquires John.

'Fifty gourdes.' Two dollars. Standard price for photographing a standard body. John starts to haggle.

'But this one was tortured before he was shot. Wounds in his face. I just told you.' The body guide is deeply offended.

'They're nearly all tortured before they're shot, kid. Thirty gourdes, take it or leave it. I can't even sell these pictures. There are better ones coming out of Rwanda.' John turns the page of his paper.

The body guides sometimes find three or four bodies a day, in the street or dumped at the side of the road, mutilated or otherwise, and they sell the secret of their location to journalists. It's a new source of income for Haitians. They hang around in hotel receptions waiting for clients and can sell the same body several times in a day, until all the journalists know where it is or the relatives have dragged it home. Petrol for the hearse has become too expensive. The dead sometimes lie in the street for days, usually somewhere in Cité Soleil, where Aristide's supporters live.

'OK, thirty,' says the body guide.

'Fancy coming along?' asks John. I thank him but no. Bodies are more photo- than radio-genic. Besides, I have to attend the American briefing to hear that the latest developments in the restoration of democracy are positive.

There are six journalists left. They have spread themselves out across the USIS room.

'We are making progress,' begins Stanley. The figure of 3,000 dead since the coup is now rising by an average of thirty a month. The number of rapes, disappearances and assaults is also increasing. This morning a pickup truck full of soldiers stopped next to the queue of asylum seekers outside the Rex. They laid about them with clubs and then drove off. Three people in the queue were seriously wounded and had to be carried away. Where to remains a mystery.

'Tip of the iceberg,' says Stanley of the official figures. A few months ago, when no invasion was being considered and human rights organizations were claiming that eighty Haitians a month were being murdered by the regime, US Ambassador Swing sent a fax to the State Department stating that left-wing human-rights guys were manipulating figures and exaggerating the brutality of the Haitian regime. Now the Americans highlight such reports, or write them themselves.

'The regime is now really starting to collapse under the pressure of the embargo,' Stanley continues into the microphones. 'We are seeing signs of division in the ranks of the military and do not rule out a revolt against Cédras.' After he delivers these difficult lines, his nails disappear between his teeth again.

The *Washington Post* closes his empty notebook. His paper, along with the rest of the world's press, is going to lead with Rwanda again. We rise from the hard wooden seat and leave the pressroom.

Outside on the pavement another reporter says cynically: 'That would suit Clinton just fine, wouldn't it, if there was an internal coup against Cédras? Save him from having to throw him out of the country himself.'

I ask Amos, one of the body guides, if this is likely, but he gives the Americans little chance of such a lucky break. Amos is worth listening to because his big brother, Gérard, is a colonel in the army.

'Gérard has been in a bad mood recently, it's true, but that's because he can't cash his salary cheque.' Haiti's National Bank still opens for business every morning at nine, but it has run out of cash.

### America tightens sanctions against Haiti
Washington, 11 June 1994 – President Clinton now hopes to bring the military regime in Haiti to its knees with a new ban on commercial flights. The final services operating to and from Haiti will

> be suspended from the end of the month. Sanctions
> are being expanded to cover commercial flights
> because it appears that the Haitian elite has con-
> tinued to buy goods in Miami. Among those
> making frequent use of the 'shuttles' has been the
> wife of General Cédras.             (*de Volkskrant*)

'Yesterday the price of beans went up three times. Last week, prices only rose twice every day. I begin to worry that *les Américains* are going to wall us up here until we're all dead,' says Maurice. He sold his only pair of shoes weeks ago for a sack of maize flour, which will probably be empty by now. I mentally run through his other possessions: the trousers and the flip-flops he's wearing, two plank beds for himself and his three children and an aluminium bucket that I once saw standing behind his front door. Apart from these I can't think of anything saleable. So that means it's going to cost me again.

Maurice was once my 'journalist guide'. The profession dates from February 1986, when hundreds of journalists descended on Port-au-Prince to cover the fall of the loathed Baby Doc Duvalier, son of the hated dictator Papa Doc Duvalier. The bulk of the correspondents had never investigated anything in Haiti before and were lost on their own. So they each employed a young anti-Duvalier Haitian to show them around and translate interviews in and out of Creole. It was dangerous work: the last Duvalier might well have left for Switzerland, but his henchmen, the Tontons Macoute, were still on the loose.

The profession flourished for three weeks back then. But it still exists, even though unemployment in the sector is almost 100 per cent. Soon after the installation of Duvalier's successor the press departed, returning faithfully for a few days every year to cover the next coup. Haiti correspondents thus gradually learned to find their own way around Port-au-Prince and most learned a few words of Creole. The guides were no longer needed, but saw that as no reason to change their careers. They believe that they still have a claim on 'their' journalists, and 'their' journalists are sensitive to this historical obligation: after all, they have served in the trenches together.

Since the embargo, the guides have exploited the old claim more desperately than ever. The French photographer Claudia has been saddled with Jean-Claude since the fall of Duvalier. He is now twenty-five and has grown from a charming street kid into a homeless cocaine addict with three children: or rather, three of whose existence he is aware. Jean-Claude is moreover crippled, having been shot during a government raid into Cité Soleil, where he often hangs out with his mates. He depends on crutches and even with them can walk only very short distances. Claudia has paid for all the operations on his legs, provides the crutches and helps feed his children.

I myself am bolted to Maurice, probably for life. I am lucky: Maurice does not sniff or booze, has not had children for twelve years and does his best to earn a few cents in my absence. He runs a languishing souvenir boutique, a clay hut crammed with battered trinkets, on the steps of Hotel Oloffson. Ever since I've known him he has been dreaming of giving the hut a coat of paint, because he is convinced that the lack of customers is due to its shabbiness. I long ago gave him the money for a pot of paint but, for as long as this regime is in charge, Maurice would rather keep it in his pocket. He knows from experience that it is better not to show that you can afford anything, not even a new colour on your walls.

I buy at least two paintings from him per visit to Haiti, plus an ornamental objet d'art in metal and three carved wooden statues. They are all of the same abominable quality, but this way I have the idea that he is giving me something in exchange for the funds I each time reserve for him and his three children.

Maurice is the most lethargic speaker in the western hemisphere and therefore unusable for radio reports. In the many lost hours we have spent together, waiting for our turn to come up in the Security Council, I have frequently tried to record his wonderful story about 'the trouble dog' on tape. You can't expect even the most committed radio audience to sit there for an hour, but I can never get Maurice to come to the point any quicker. Here it is, therefore, in essence.

One beautiful day in the year 1980, Maurice is standing on the quayside in Port-au-Prince watching the departure of a cruise ship full of American tourists en route for the Bahamas. At that time Haiti was still one of the top ten tourist destinations, and ten cruise ships a day were calling at the 'Pearl of the Caribbean'. The ship is already a few hundred metres off shore when Maurice sees something slip from the arm of an elderly American lady, who is standing waving on deck. It hits the sea and begins to swim for shore. A dog! The animal will never make it, thinks Maurice, and he jumps in to save it. Which he does. But back on dry land, what an ugly dog it turns out to be. Strange little short legs, long hair, dripping wet of course, and a stupid flat muzzle, with at least as flat a nose, through which the creature can only breathe with great difficulty. At this point, if the story is well told, the listener realizes that it's a Pekinese, probably the first and last specimen to set foot on Haitian soil. Here you mainly find scrawny mongrels hobbling round on three legs, crawling with fleas and covered with mange.

Maurice takes the Pekinese home to his shack in the alley and expects it to do what Haitian dogs do: namely, scratch a living on the streets. But when Maurice opens the door for him in the morning, the Pekinese simply looks at him in total surprise. Culture shock, or troubled by the heat, Maurice thinks, so he tries it again for a couple of days and then takes the trouble to show the dog how you get something to eat in Haiti. He serves up a delicious pile of garbage, but the Pekinese simply does not grasp that the orange peel and split mango stones are meant to be eaten. The animal begins to starve.

'This dog trouble dog,' Maurice finally realizes. 'He die if he stay with me.' So he spends many days searching for a more suitable milieu. It is touch and go whether the creature will starve to death first. But at the very last minute Maurice finds the director of the Pepsi-Cola Company in Port-au-Prince prepared to take the dog on. Pepsi was still doing business in Haiti in those days.

The owner of the Pekinese never came back to look for it. In 1981 AIDS was discovered and Americans thought that all Haitians had it. Tourism in Haiti was finished.

Before he packs up my souvenirs with cardboard and string, Maurice dusts them off carefully. 'Mees Leenda' deserves the best of the best. Indeed, I have to be cherished. Although he's five years older than me, he manages to call me his *mère*. No wonder. I keep him alive. Not that I'm happy with this honorary title, far from it. Two visits to Haiti ago I felt so guilty about leaving him behind when I left that, along with a colleague, I bought him a real pig. 'Pigs are moneybox. Big pigs get little pigs. Whenever you need money, you sell little pig,' Maurice had explained to me shortly before.

I asked him to call his pig 'Leenda'. He looked at me as if I'd gone mad and cried, '*Jamais!*' A greater insult directed at his *mère* could not be imagined. A pity. The pig was christened Mathilda instead.

I am also responsible for keeping Mathilda alive, of course. When I next reported to Maurice, Mathilda had had trouble with worms and there was a vet's bill awaiting me: 250

gourdes, or $10. Today Maurice is complaining that Mathilda has escaped. She has torn herself loose from the rope and devoured the last few potatoes belonging to the neighbours. These have brought her to the local attaché and Maurice will have to pay a fine of fifty gourdes to get her back. I fish the money out of my trouser pocket.

France apparently thinks that blue helmets will be found for Rwanda after all, and is going ahead with the preparatory phase of the UN mission: the French invasion.

### France threatens military intervention in Rwanda

Paris, 16 June 1994 – If the blood baths in Rwanda continue and a cease-fire agreed on Tuesday is not respected, France and her 'most important European and African allies' are prepared to intervene militarily. Precisely which countries these will be, Paris is not yet in a position to announce. French Foreign Minister Juppé made known that he had yesterday proposed to Boutros-Ghali that 2–3,000 UN soldiers be 'immediately' flown to Rwanda from the mission in Somalia. French President Mitterrand also declared that two or three African countries had reacted positively to French requests for troops to take part in the intervention. 'I am still waiting for clear answers from the European countries. But whoever else may be involved, we will do it. Every hour counts.'

(Reuters, AFP)

And there's also news for us in Haiti.

**ALM suspends flights to Haiti**
Port-au-Prince, 21 June 1994 – ALM, the Dutch-
Antilles airline, the last company still flying in and
out of Haiti, will fly its last service between Haiti
and the US this coming Wednesday, departing
from Curaçao at 13.25.                                    (AP)

When the tarmac roads degenerated into muddy tracks, the
MREs bought Jeeps. And when the telephones cut out, they
went over to walkie-talkies. The junta and their cronies are a
resilient lot. Now that the final flights to Miami have been
suspended, the elite is on the lookout for new forms of amusement. The advertisement section of *Le Nouvelliste* is full of
courses offering Salsa dancing and Spanish conversation. And
on Friday evenings, up in Pétionville, the car park of the El
Rancho casino is still full of four-wheel drives. I even have to
squeeze between a couple of Porsches as I wander up to the
entrance.

Around the splashing fountain of the swimming pool,
couples dance carefree tangos. The ladies drink cola, but
exclusively light: MREs are still having to watch their weight.
I wave to a couple of US Embassy staff, before taking my
place at the table with colleagues. We order lobster. Grégoire
Ahmad, who is swirling his partner along the edge of the
pool, frees himself from her arms and comes over, grinning
triumphantly: 'So you write all about MREs, but you sit
scoffing lobster like us. You are all MRJs,' he scoffs. Morally
Repugnant Journalists. Touché. These days we go down to
Kuwait City late in the day, when the hawkers are hungry
enough to offload their contraband petrol at knock-down
prices. The border with the Dominican Republic is now
patrolled by the UN and there is suddenly less *gaz* available in
Haiti. The casino's air-conditioning no longer works – no

fuel for the generators. So they're feeling the pinch just a bit up in Pétionville. Panting gamblers pull the fruit machines and then slump into armchairs under the chandeliers. A young MRE with pimply cheeks, his deathly bored girlfriend perched on a stool beside him, throws one 500 gourde note after another on to the roulette table and keeps losing.

Down in Cité Soleil, voodoo flags flap above a sea of corrugated iron roofs. But people also trudge round with bibles. The words '*Viv Eternel*' are chalked on the streets and the taptaps are covered with paintings of Jesus and the Apostles. Slum-dwellers seek help from wherever they can get it.

Photographer John and I park next to a water-pump. The car immediately fills with bluebottles. A queue of women waiting for water loops around two bodies. They are stretched out next to each other in a patch of dried blood. Their hands are tied behind their backs. The alley is narrow: the heads of the dead men are almost inside the living room of a woman who is taking curlers out of her hair. As John takes pictures and I take notes, several people stop to look. At us, not at the bodies.

'Who are they?' I ask no one in particular. The woman with the curlers shrugs her shoulders.

'Chiclets?' says a passing chewing-gum seller.

'How long have they been lying here?'

'Cigarette? Cigarette?' asks another street trader.

The only ambulance in Port-au-Prince, a dented and bumperless wreck from the Hôpital Général, comes jolting through the potholes and parks under a billboard displaying a cock in a chef's hat: an advert for chicken stockcubes. The driver gets out and loosens the wire that holds up the tailgate. He has knotted a handkerchief over his nose and mouth. There is already one body lying in the back, thin and dusty, as if it had come from Somalia. With the help of bystanders, the two dead men are thrown on top of it.

When we arrive back at the Oloffson, a disturbing fin de siècle feeling steals over me. The remnants of a cold buffet are being carried back to the kitchen. A rented chamber orchestra is playing Mozart. The sinking of the *Titanic* was also accompanied by chamber music, I seem to remember. I am also worried about Mathilda. The junta may still be holding out, but Maurice's piggy bank is threatening to succumb to the embargo. She can no longer find enough garbage to eat. People are getting there first. I sent Maurice off to the market this morning with some cash for a sack of nutritious pigfood, if it is to be had. He has still not returned.

A Dutch photographer is just scraping the last morsels of griot, pieces of grilled pork, from his plate. 'You should have heard the other photographers,' he laughs. Dusty and tired from their daily search for bodies in the slums, they had come on to the hotel veranda and found the Dutchman stuffing himself. 'What! Are you still eating pork?' they had cried in amazement. They had just seen a pig tucking into a dead baby that had been dumped on the street.

### French invasion begins today

Paris, 23 June 1994 – The French Ministry of Defence has announced that Opération Turquoise, the French intervention in Rwanda, is already underway. Troops from the Foreign Legion and the French marines, in armoured vehicles and with helicopter cover, will enter western Rwanda from Zaire. The invasion force will pull out again in two months, on 22 August. A UN peacekeeping force will then take over the mission.         (Reuters)

Blue helmets to follow the invasion of Rwanda have still not been found.

Meanwhile, back in Haiti, the regime is not giving an inch. Today General Cédras and his wife are attending Mass in a pretty white church in the centre of town. It goes without saying: the man is deeply religious.

Journalists are not allowed in. Burly bodyguards in black balaclavas keep pushing us back. They call themselves 'the ninjas'. We are condemned to wait on the steps, in the burning sun and beset by beggars, until the service is over.

For the few journalists who remain in Haiti, Cédras's attendance at church is the only opportunity to see him. For the rest of the week the General hides himself away in the Quartier Général. If I stand on my toes, I can just see over the bodyguards and glimpse the back of his head. He is sitting in the front pew. The church is packed. Little girls in lace dresses play tag in the aisle. The choir performs Gregorian music and six priests officiate round the altar.

Finally the congregation begins to leave the church, to the strains of Handel's *Messiah*, with orchestra. The priests are the first to emerge; the photographers surge forward. Then comes Cédras, sailing down the steps hand in hand with his wife Yannick. She has a pearl tiara perched on her hairdo. The General laughs, waves and shakes a few hands. To my annoyance, I see a man whose nights are patently not disturbed by thoughts of an imminent invasion. Bodyguards shepherd the couple to the waiting car. Photographers stumble after them. Cédras shakes another hand. Questions are not answered. The press is roughly pushed aside.

Against the front wheel of the Cédrases' snow-white Land Rover sits a beggar woman in filthy rags, her hair stiff with dust. A baby is encrusted to her arms. When the engine of the royal *voiture* bursts into life, she does not react. Someone drags her away just before she is run over.

The photographers briefly chase after the car, but it is a lost cause. The driver accelerates, water from the broken mains sprays up from the tyres and, horn braying, the vehicle disappears round the corner.

Aubelin is not bluffing: the Cédrases are indeed planning their political future in Haiti. A group of labourers are shovelling sand and earth from the roadside into deep potholes, when a little election caravan of three cars, led by the Cédrases' Land Rover, pulls up beside them. The ninjas leap out, balaclavas and machine guns at the ready. The labourers bolt in terror. The ninjas scream at them to stay right where they are – the General only wants to give them some money, the traditional alms of a Haitian president to his people. The men come back trembling. They accept the coins and then take to their heels again. Their shovels are left abandoned in the road.

Late in the evening, and I'm walking back to the Prestige through the deserted streets. The electricity is off again and it's pitch-dark. Two delivery vans come up behind me. Uzi barrels protrude from the windows. The vans slow to my pace and I am stared at by heads wearing sunglasses. The word Teleco is painted on the doors. For lack of their own equipment, the death squads operate at night using telephone company vans.

'*Bonsoir*,' barks one of the men.

'*Bonsoir, bonsoir*,' I reply with manic jollity. The vans drive on.

Two streets further up I hear the rattle of the same Uzis.

★

This morning Toto has managed to find the veranda of the Oloffson. Next to him at the breakfast table sits the FRAPH number two, a fat man called Jojo. He watches with interest as the boss pricks the yolk of his fried egg with a fork. I'm bored at the press table. The World Cup has kicked off in the good ol' US of A and the guys are talking football. So I go and interview Toto instead.

'How are you going to defend yourselves when the Americans invade?' I ask.

Toto is delighted with the question. He pulls me down by the sleeve until my ear virtually disappears between his lips and whispers: 'Black magic.' There is an impressively long silence and then he goes on: 'They will have to be very careful what they eat and drink in Haiti. Good chance that we will have poisoned it. There are voodoo powders ready in every local FRAPH office. Some of them can make the Haitian army invisible. We've got AIDS in powder form. And we're also rapidly developing a very special treat. I've already tried out the prototype on my dog. One lick and the animal flew up to the ceiling and then dropped down dead at my feet.'

'Wow!' I say, trying to sound impressed.

'Yes, you better believe it. So if the Americans come they'd better bring a good supply of body bags with them. I've been trying to warn the American Embassy of the risks, but Stanley Schrager refuses to see me. Stupid, stupid, stupid.'

I thank Toto and head for Stanley. He doesn't know anything about Toto's offer to negotiate but everything about their strategic plans. 'I recently met a senior Haitian officer in a bar up in Pétionville. He came up to me and said: "If you invade, you will be sorry." "And what will you be?" I asked him. "We will be dead," he said. "Well," I said, "I'd rather be sorry than dead."'

'When's the invasion, Stan?'

'Soon. At least, if it's necessary. We are keeping all options open,' he replies, and saunters off sniffing hard.

**America still on its own with invasion plan**
The problem is, that nobody else is enthusiastic about an invasion to drive out the military junta in Haiti. France is against it and Foreign Minister Juppé has already announced that he is not willing to make French troops available. Within the Security Council, Russia and China are also against it. Washington has not yet secured more than informal commitments from Argentina, Chile, Costa Rica and a few Caribbean islands. That creates problems, because . . . the US government can only proceed with an invasion when a UN peacekeeping force for Haiti is in place.

(*de Volkskrant*, 13 July 1994)

This morning Stanley has to admit it. In spite of the negligible risk of dying in Operation Restore Democracy, the campaign to recruit participants is proving disappointing. But before unveiling the figures he instructs us to regard the number of non-American soldiers recruited to serve in the first part of the operation, the invasion itself, as 'symbolic'. The multi-national invasion force will be precisely 20,266 strong: 20,000 from the US and 266 from neighbouring Jamaica, Barbados, Belize and Trinidad. These troops are now in Puerto Rico being given American training in marksmanship, first aid, radio communications and riot control.

The recruitment of blue helmets is faring even worse. In Europe the UN have drawn a total blank. Clinton is being punished via the UN for his refusal to get involved in Bosnia. In London the UN Secretary-General is told that Britain must alas forgo involvement in Haiti, 'because of the pressure of commitments in Bosnia'. In Paris he hears of heavy French commitments in Bosnia and Rwanda and is told to tell Washington that a few French troops would not influence the result of a battle for Haiti.

Member State Israel, after prolonged nagging, will send some observers. Brazil has put a few transport ships in the UN pot and Panama has agreed to send an unspecified number of doctors and nurses for the blue helmets, who have not yet been found. Surinam is still thinking about it. The only firm commitments come from Antigua, Barbuda, Guyana and Tunisia, each of which has agreed to send a handful of blue helmets.

Luckily there are always Pakistan and Bangladesh. Once again they are desperate to be included. America is happy. The invasion can go ahead.

### Security Council agrees to invasion of Haiti

New York, 31 July 1994 – The UN Security Council has approved American military intervention in Haiti. Operation Restore Democracy will be followed by the UN peacekeeping mission Uphold Democracy. Boutros-Ghali recommends a peacekeeping force of 15,000 men. America says that 4,000 will be enough. Of the more than 62 million dollars promised by Member States for the reconstruction of Haiti after the invasion, less than 10 million have been received by the UN.

Russia has threatened to block any US intervention in Haiti with its UN Security Council veto unless the administration, through the Security Council, endorses Moscow's intervention in

Georgia. Moscow has been working to add Georgia to a network of former Soviet states. The Security Council endorsed Russia's project.

'At the very least, the principle of neutrality is being diluted,' said a US official. 'It is far from ideal. But rather than not be able to do anything, we have to swallow a less-than-perfect situation.'

(*Washington Post*)

That night a low-flying American plane passes back and forth over Port-au-Prince. Next morning we find thousands of pamphlets in the streets in the morning. 'Prepare for liberation!' is the message, along with drawings of the bananas and eggs which it advises Haitians to hoard. Most people's mouths simply water on seeing the pictures.

Cédras has also been preparing for action, I see. A line of sandbags now surrounds his headquarters. Before the day is out most of the bags have been flattened by traffic. The rest have been shaken empty and stolen to carry the mangoes or turn into vests for the children.

## 3. The UN in Haiti:
## Blue Helmets without Blue Helmets

*I*

*Haiti, September 1994*

'Monday morning, nine o'clock sharp.' A radiant Stanley invites us to come and watch the invasion on 19 September 1994. The USIS room is full to bursting: my colleagues are through with Rwanda and have returned to Haiti en masse. 'You'll find the best camera positions on the public gallery next to the runway. Have a nice day.' Stanley is almost singing, interspersed with long sensual sniffs.

On Monday morning, at ten seconds past nine, American Black Hawk helicopters rise like a swarm of wasps from aircraft carriers out in the bay and swoop towards the airport. The leaves of the mango trees flanking the runway are ripped off by the wind from the rotors and whirled round for hundreds of metres. The noise is deafening. The doors spring open and out tumbles the 10th Mountain Division, who roll over flat on their bellies in a cloud of dust and litter, the sights of their automatic weapons clamped to their eyes.

'What a pity,' says a fellow journalist. We are using the points of our T-shirts to pick bits of dirt out of each other's eyes. 'All down safely. That was the riskiest moment of the whole operation. When they invaded Panama, twenty-three GIs managed to break a leg jumping out of the choppers.'

Even at this early hour the temperature has risen to 33°C with 100 per cent humidity. The 10th Mountain almost sink to their knees as they wrench themselves upright on the soft, shimmering asphalt. Their packs are heavy as lead and, thanks to the bullet-proof breastplates that stretch from their chins to halfway down their thighs, they can hardly put one foot in front of the other. A couple roll over and for a moment are stranded as helpless as turtles. While the helicopters turn and zoom furiously back to the ships, a handful of assault troops, top-heavy as unhorsed knights, trudge up below us towards the arrival hall, weapons thrust out before them like battering rams.

'Hi there, Linda!' comes a cry from the runway. I don't believe it. It is Freddy from the 10th Mountain unit in Mogadishu. So it was 'first Haiti and then Bosnia' for him after all.

'Hey, Freddy! Hi!' I wave back. 'Come up here for a minute, soldier!'

Freddy gestures to ears tucked deep into his huge helmet, shrugs his bullet-proof shoulders apologetically and points forward. I get it. He can't hear me and he has to go and capture customs. He joins the assault before I can mime him to take it easy: the authorities surrendered half an hour ago. I saw the customs officers sitting on the pavement outside at half past eight this morning. 'What are you feeling?' I had asked them on the way in.

'*Rien du tout*,' replied one of them, head down.

'Hands up!' says Freddy's voice from downstairs to nobody in particular.

'If we start after breakfast, we'll be finished by lunchtime,' was the Pentagon's prediction for the conquest of Haiti. They must have meant it literally. At about half past nine the first of what will soon become an endless stream of transport helicopters lands bearing herds of construction workers from Brown & Root. They immediately set about digging latrines beside the runway and hammering thousands of tent pegs into

Haiti's hard ground. In the hours which follow ever more construction workers prise open ever more crates full of tents, while an impressive fleet of tanks and trucks appears from the holds of a procession of Hercules transport planes.

When I return just before lunch to check on the progress of Operation Restore Democracy, it's like I'm back in Somalia with Continue Hope. Port Base Mogadishu is being shaken out of American containers almost intact. Familiar mortar nets flap over the tents in the warm wind, and the same rolls of barbed wire keep the new natives at a safe distance. As each container is opened, Somali dust and sand swirl into the air. In the rush to leave Somalia, Port was never swept out.

Just before the invasion, Clinton's negotiators arrived in Port-au-Prince and said to the junta leaders, 'Look, America has decided to restore democracy here. If you don't co-operate we'll pulverize you.' The Haitian army seems to have got the message: the few Haitian soldiers who turned up for work in the harbour this morning have obediently handed over their weapons. They are now standing on the quayside in scared little groups, between rapidly rising stacks of cases and crates. They stare open-mouthed towards the sea, where lines of nuclear-powered warships stand off awaiting a berth. More than 20,000 men and their equipment are swung ashore, plus a few sacks of food aid. The Americans are hoping to pacify potentially hostile natives by handing out food.

The GIs standing guard behind the harbour fence have tied handkerchiefs over their faces to keep out the stench of the open drains. I am about to interview them through the railings – 'I come from Alabama, ma'am' – when we see a wave of slum-dwellers surging out of the main alley of Cité Soleil on to Boulevard la Saline. The wave begins to roll towards us. The eyes of the Haitian soldiers on the quay bulge with panic.

They rush to find somewhere to hide, the best place being behind broad American backs. But the Americans push the local soldiers away to find quick cover themselves.

Without taking his eyes off the pitiful creatures approaching him, the GI from Alabama feels for the weapon that hangs from the belt round his steel-plated belly. Then he rips away his handkerchief and reveals himself as a pimply adolescent.

'Who are those people?' he gasps.

'Slum-dwellers,' I reply. His finger tightens on the trigger. Too late I realize that in the American mind the word 'slum' evokes visions of murderous gangs.

'What do they want?'

'To welcome you,' I reassure him. His colleagues are busy disappearing behind containers and levelling their weapons.

'You sure of that? Can you understand what they're screaming?' The US Army has not yet unpacked the Creole translators.

The vanguard of the ragged procession has now approached to within 50 metres of the fence. I listen: 'They are screaming that the Haitian army is *caca* – that means shit – and that they want to have Aristide back, and the sooner the better,' I translate for him.

'Who?' asks the GI.

'Aristide,' I say. The American looks at me in total incomprehension.

The fittest have now reached the fence and are climbing the railings acrobatically. A few hundred enthusiastic dancers have soon gathered at its base and are hopping up and down.

'Back! Back!' screams the American soldier.

'*Liberté, Merci Beel Cling Dong!*' scream back the Haitians.

'What are they shouting? What are they shouting?' the soldier demands, but the Haitians drag me away from the fence to join a wild dance of joy. The Americans are meanwhile enthusiastically waved at with palm fronds, with yellowed photos of Aristide, and with terrified roosters, a tribute previously reserved exclusively for Aristide himself, the fighting cock being his former campaign symbol. To mark the occasion, many people have also dragged out tea cosies, clipped into cockscombs, and donned them for the first time since the 1991 elections.

I wrestle myself back to the fence. The soldier is still standing there shouting 'Back! Back!' And then yells to me: 'Why are these people wearing tea cosies on their heads?'

'They are cockscombs,' I begin to explain, but he interrupts: 'Some kinda voodoo?'

He begins to calm down when a line of BMWs and Mitsubishis appears and begins to file past in the rear. Where he comes from the owners of vehicles like these are respectable citizens. But in Haiti they are the MREs and the rent-a-mob managers, who have come down the hill to watch the restoration of democracy from behind tinted glass. With their windows up and air-conditioning on to keep out the stench of the slums.

'Those are the real bad guys,' I explain, uninvited. 'In Haiti you find the gangs in the smart neighbourhoods, not in the slums.'

'Back! Back!' screams the soldier from Alabama. And this time I am included.

An endless procession of trucks passes out through the harbour gate and turns into the filthy Boulevard la Saline. They are taking millions of litres of American drinking water and petrol to the US Army camps that are springing up all over the city. The convoys of tankers manoeuvre past the dump-trucks and asphalt-layers of the Brown & Root arsenal. The few supply routes that the US Army thinks it will need while restoring democracy are rapidly cleared of compacted garbage and, where drains have been blocked since living memory, drained.

'Hey, this is great!' shouts a digger operator. 'We're finding a layer of asphalt under this muck, maybe put down by the Romans. The garbage has fossilized here. We'll be striking oil soon!'

A small crowd watch as the throbbing machines uncover a long-forgotten road. One of the workmen, encouraged by admiring faces, sings 'O Sole Mio' for the spectators.

This evening, as before, the combos parade past the packed terrace of Cindy's Place, while under the only working street lamp the child whores exhibit themselves as usual. The bars and restaurants of Pétionville, high above the invasion, have opened their doors as if nothing has happened and are immediately swarming with customers – MREs enthusiastically exchanging eye-witness reports.

'If you leave them alone, they leave you alone, that's what I've noticed,' I overhear from the next table.

'While they're here, you can do good business with them. Just this afternoon there was an American major on the pavement outside, pleading to rent storage space. I signed a ridiculous contract with him!' someone else says proudly.

The press corps also meet up at Cindy's, dazed but delighted with the US Army's spectacular entrée. Dinner is ordered.

'They've taken control of the Quartier Général. Just walked in,' reports Reuters.

'Tonight they're heading up north to take Cap-Haitien,' or so the *Miami Herald* has heard.

We glance up from our plates as an American patrol prowls past the tables, the first American forces to have located Pétionville. They are in square formation, so that all flanks are covered. The soldier charged with the rear is obliged to walk backwards. His buddies have linked arms and are pulling him behind them. For a moment our eyes meet. In his, doubt: 'Do I look a total asshole walking backwards through all you good-timers? Or are you all snipers in disguise as good-timers?' The patrol disappears round the corner.

'More wine anybody?' asks one of my colleagues.

It is as if all the cruise ships of old have returned to Haiti together. When I head back down the hill to the Prestige Hotel the number of brilliantly lit vessels out in the bay has still not reduced, while all over Port-au-Prince the floodlights are already magically shining on fully equipped tent camps. You can hear the drone of the generators. The street children, like chicks in an incubator, cluster in pools of American light.

Brand new American satellite dishes stand on the roof of Haiti's national TV station. Rolling texts now appear on everyone's screens: 'Stay calm. The invasion force is here for humanitarian reasons. You will be getting a better life.' Courtesy of Stan's department, the United States Information Service.

'Beautiful Stanley' Schrager really is almost beautiful this morning. He shines as if he were the Beacon of Democracy itself. Cheeks flushed with invasion fever, he laces the briefing with all the Pentagon jargon he has picked up so far. Port-au-Prince he calls 'Pap', just like the military strategists. The Haitian army is 'Fad', short for Forces Armées d'Haiti, an official name long ago replaced in Haiti by the more appropriate 'murderers', but now revived from American archives.

Stanley presents various guest speakers with broad shoulders, crew cuts, square chins and senior positions in the US Army. One such officer facing our microphones from the USIS podium this morning is already assessing Restore

Democracy as 'as good as done': 'Our victory in Haiti will go down in history as the easiest ever. We have christened it "The Velvet Invasion". Not a shot fired, not a drop of blood spilled,' says the General, grinning broadly.

He has marked red areas on the map of Pap that adorns Stanley's wall. These are the places where Camp Dragon, Camp Falcon, Camp Muleskinner, Camp Super and Camp Democracy have been knocked up by Brown & Root overnight. He now invites us to come and witness America disarming the 'Fad' (or at least, the 'Fad' unit that keeps conducting coups) with our own eyes.

'An historic event,' says Stanley, 'at eleven hundred hours. You can take photos.'

'*Honneur. Discipline. Compétence*', the motto of the Haitian army, is inscribed on a bronze plaque above the gate of Camp d'Application. It too is in Pétionville. In most of the innumerable *coups d'état*, the guns have rolled out of these barracks and down to the Presidential Palace *là-bas*. The gates are now firmly locked. It is two minutes before 11.00 hours.

'No parking here,' snarls a Haitian soldier as we pull up in front of the building.

'Really? The Americans said it would be OK,' bluffs John the photographer.

'Oh . . . I see . . .' says the soldier hesitantly and backs off. I almost feel sorry for him. Yesterday he could have just shot us, had he happened to feel like it. Today it is the Americans who decide what he can and can't do.

The poor man is also superfluous to the ceremonial disarming of his unit: at 11.00 hours precisely American helicopters simply fly over the closed gates and land on Camp d'Application's parade ground. The soldier has to frantically find his key and unlock the gates in order to be there on time. Without a murmur, the 'Fad' assist in assembling their weapons. The modest collection is already laid out awaiting confiscation.

'What will you do with them?' I ask an American officer.

'Decommission 'em,' he replies. 'Not destroy 'em. That would be a waste. Those jeeps with no wheels are just junk, sure, but some of these guns ought to be in a museum back home. They're collectors' items, probably used in the Second World War.'

It is not the restoration of democracy that I am witnessing. It is the American Army (and its sidekick Brown & Root) erecting, at breathtaking speed, the set for a movie about democracy. They are rapidly throwing together an illusion designed to distract the eye from reality. The Americans would like nothing better than to be finished in Haiti before Thanksgiving in November, so that UN troops can take over. That's around eight weeks away.

Day and night, the Americans seems to be working their way through a list of 'props required for a Democratic Republic'. Top of the list: a Presidential Palace. Without which the set will not look real enough.

American tanks roll up to the twisted gates of the old Palace gardens on the Champs de Mars. The Haitian soldiers on guard behind the railings shrink back in horror. Nobody on earth can stand up to this flashing and roaring machinery, certainly not these gatekeepers, whose rolling stock has long been confined to a few bicycles. One of them disappears between the unkempt bushes, while the others stand rooted to the spot.

The shaven head of an American sergeant appears from the tank turret. 'Good morning, gentlemen. We are taking over from you here. Gates open, please.' The words are polite, but all the Haitians understand is the tone in which they are spoken. With trembling hands they grope in their pockets for the keys.

Driving in behind the tanks come Brown & Root. Tailgates drop and cases in military green are lugged up the marble steps, while Haitian soldiers slip down them as inconspicuously as possible.

Parliament and ministries, the next items on the American list, are already empty when the Liberators drive up. Cédras's officials moved out days before the invasion, taking with them everything that was not nailed to the floor. Telephones, faxes, table lamps, chairs and tables have all disappeared. So have the curtains: American contractors wearing paint-spattered caps have just hung up new ones in the Senate, and there are ladders standing against the façade of the Parliament building. From inside comes the sound of hammering and sawing. Immediately following the invasion, the Americans have put out an appeal to Aristide's officials to come out of hiding and get on with governing. At home they are tracking down officials to whom they had given post-coup asylum and flying them back to Haiti as soon as they find them.

I come across a group of American soldiers rocking on old kitchen chairs in front of the Parliament building. They are gazing nonplussed at some Haitians, who are giving a new coat of paint to a blistered fountain by the entrance. The graceful mermaids round the basin have been painted a uniform bright blue. Another pot seems to hold pink lacquer, the colour of seaside-rock. With this they now daub the stone fish, which rise mouths agape from the centre of the pool. The fountain has been dry for years and is now full of rubbish and excrement.

I ask the soldiers whether the appeal for Aristide's people

to come back and govern has had any success. 'We don't know for sure, ma'am, but we think so. There are a few locals inside having a meeting right now. They could be something to do with the government,' says one soldier hopefully. He can already smell that Thanksgiving turkey back home.

Legal proceedings against Raoul Cédras, Michel François and Philippe Biamby, the military Band of Three, are not strictly necessary: the Americans simply erase them from the democracy they are now busy staging. 'We will leave the regime to the judgement of history,' declares Stanley.

The world is still dripping from a tropical downpour as the 'Saddams' take off in an American plane bound for Panama, their chosen destination. I watch them until they disappear in the clouds.

On the way back to the Prestige, I stumble into Haitians who have set up house under bits of cardboard on top of the garbage thrown over the fence by GIs who are camped at the airport. I watch them fight over opened mini-packs of peanut butter and strawberry jam. Here and there people test discarded lithium batteries (probably the first of their kind in Haiti) with their tongues.

'President Clinton's foreign policy is working,' concludes Stanley.

The Band of Three has barely left the stage when ships from the US Coastguard, full to the gunwhales with bot pippel, dock in Port-au-Prince. The sleek vessels squeeze between the warships and unload the Guantánamo refugees on the crumbling quay. The camp in Cuba is now being emptied as quickly as possible, in shipments of several hundred bot pippel a day. Now, thanks to the invasion, Clinton's refugee policy is also a success.

**Clinton thanks UN**

New York, 27 September 1994 – In a speech yesterday to the General Assembly, President Clinton thanked the UN for its support and contribution to the restoration of democracy in Haiti. According to Clinton, the UN has a special role to play in spreading and strengthening democracy worldwide. He sees recent events in Haiti as an outstanding example of multilateral co-operation.

(Reuters)

The embargo on air travel to and from Haiti has been lifted. In the departure hall, passengers step cautiously over the American sleeping bags spread out on the floor. Freddy, the Somalia veteran, is still billeted here with his unit. I find him helmeted up behind a pile of car tyres on the pavement in front of customs. I've already invited him several times for a night out at the casino, lobster *compris*, but he has not been allowed off the airport since landing. Around Freddy and his buddies there is a small but permanent crowd, silently staring. A scraggy dog comes snuffling round between the people's legs and lifts its leg against Freddy's barricade. 'Fuck off,' he hisses to discourage the animal. Some of the bystanders back away in dismay.

Maurice is one of them. To him these Americans are the most interesting of the 20,000 who have descended on Haiti. A piece of the asphalt in front of the departure hall has been dug up and GIs are hard at work filling sandbags from the hole. Maurice has never seen a *blanc* doing physical labour before. In Haitian society, the white masters get their heavy work done by black slaves.

'Why are they working? Wouldn't they do better getting me to do it? For a few gourdes?' Maurice sounds genuinely surprised.

'It's like a fucking zoo here, man,' complains Freddy, when I ask him how he's getting on in Haiti. His eyes shoot from one group of ragged Haitians to another. Maurice is one of the few wearing shoes. Most of them have to get by with mud socks. Tattered T-shirts hang on skinny bodies and babies hang on withered, naked breasts. As they feed, some of the women balance buckets of muddy drinking water on their heads. Lack of money has made people creative: all over the city the water mains have been dug out of the ground, sometimes straight through the asphalt. Holes are then drilled in the pipes and the supply tapped for free.

'They stare at us, from early in the morning to late at night, saying nothing, just standing there looking at every movement we make. It's making me edgy.' Freddy sniffs deeply and shudders. 'It smells just like Somalia, don't you think?'

I sniff politely. 'Mmmm, well, a bit I suppose.' Actually I don't agree. Haiti smells much worse than Somalia, but I don't want to make Freddy even more nervous.

'Just look at those vacant stares. Don't they have nothing better to do? I reckon they got a lot of ground to make up if they want it to look like a real democracy. Why don't they go lay some drains or something?'

Maurice appears at my side. Freddy's finger tightens round the trigger.

'Tell this American that I will fill up those sandbags for only five gourdes,' Maurice instructs me in Creole. One dollar. Freddy doesn't understand and looks at him with a mixture of disgust and compassion.

'How can people be so filthy . . . ?' he sighs.

Haiti is slowly turning into a showcase for the world's largest arms manufacturer and dealer. Haitians who get in the way of the military's set-building can expect to face demonstrations of the very latest gadgets. From the 'non-lethal range', we have weapons which leave the enemy helpless but alive. Guns which fire stuff that immediately disables car engines. An explosive gas, the world's most powerful light-bulb, which can blind whole crowds in a flash. A machine that produces low frequency 'infra sound' and allows American soldiers to induce epileptic fits in the populace. I had already read about this hellish sound machine in a fax at the Oloffson, but now I can see it being aimed at me. It looks like an ordinary hi-fi speaker. I have joined Maurice and a few hundred companions celebrating their way through the streets. Days after the invasion and the congas are still snaking around the American camps. We spot a patrol crossing the Champs de Mars in an armoured vehicle and caper over in their direction, singing. The Americans see us coming. Their immediate reaction, as usual, is to shout 'Back! Back!' at us through megaphones. But we don't listen and instead try to decorate their APC antennae with inflated condoms. A window rolls down and a little loudspeaker appears. With a last spiteful glance at us, the driver turns a knob on the dashboard. The new weapon is just as humane as the brochures claim: before the epileptic fits can begin, we can't help running away. The sound waves make us deaf and physically sick at the same time.

Palace, ministries and parliament have been captured. The Band of Three has been polished away. The Haitian army has had its wings clipped and is, for the moment, in no state to mount any coups. The shopping list is therefore complete, as is the film set around which Jean-Bertrand Aristide, as President, is supposed to wander. While he is receiving the order to pack his bags in Washington, Brown & Root are assembling a bullet-proof shield for him at the top of the Palace steps. It is as high as a man and several metres long. 'Just in case,' says a Brown & Rooter.

The *grand nettoyage* comes as an unpleasant surprise to the Americans. This is a bit of Haitian folklore that involves dozens of broom teams. It last happened in the days preceding Aristide's first installation as President.

'You don't receive the messiah on a garbage tip,' explains Maurice. He sets about his souvenirs with a duster, while out on the street years of old junk are swept into piles by the combined forces of the poor. The Americans first watch in amazement and then join in. In order not to hold up the democratizing schedule, the assembled garbage is quickly transported to out-of-town dumps in Brown & Root trucks. If it had been left to the wooden wheelbarrows that the Haitians were using, the *nettoyage* would have taken months.

The mops are out and the gutters emptied in even the filthiest slums. And then the clean city is decorated: brightly coloured American garbage and discarded Coke tins are strung on ropes and festooned over streets or tied to the Palace gates. The streets themselves are transformed into art galleries. People collect stones, chalk them white and then lay them out to form words. 'Tank you P. Clingtong' I read on the pavement in front of the Palace. The walls of houses are covered from top to bottom with frescos. Most depict huge Aristides, God-like in long white robes, sharing out bread and wine. Aristide's gamecock, the 'Kok Kalité', is everywhere painted in fluorescent colours, often with a baseball bat under one wing to make the point.

'Aristide for 50 years' has been painted in cheerfully dancing letters on the Palace wall. And to ensure that he lasts half a century without being murdered, someone has added 'USA please stay for 50 years'.

The American soldiers who have been camped in the Palace gardens ever since the invasion, look on appalled at the new graffiti. 'Lord have mercy,' begs one of them. 'Fifty days, man, and I've had it.'

'I don't exactly know what we've restored here, but it sure ain't democracy. I already told you, man. They just don't get the fuckin' point,' says his buddy nervously.

The poor patch up their last good trousers and the rich barricade themselves in their villas behind steel gates, beneath which scrape the whining muzzles of their Dobermans. Pap is ready for it. Tele Haiti carries live pictures of Aristide's plane taking off from Washington and follows the aircraft until it is a spot of which nothing remains.

Ninety minutes later and they turn on the cameras in Port-au-Prince. The spot reappears and turns back into a gleaming plane. Fritz, the receptionist at the Prestige, stands behind the desk watching the pictures on TV. He clutches the trembling hand of his friend, the cleaner. Tears spring to their eyes as the plane touches down on Haitian soil. They bite their lips. They don't dare to weep with joy openly: the Ahmads too are glued to the screen, rocking furiously.

'If he ever comes home, Aristide will be flat-assed broke without even a pot to piss in,' an aid worker had once predicted to me. He was right: even the toilet bowls have been stolen from the Palace. There is no computer for the President, almost no working telephone lines and no chair left to sit on. Empty and half-empty packing cases, left behind by the regime, still stand in the corridors. The water has been cut off. Thus the leader of the world's newest democracy has to make do with water in aluminium buckets that he has borrowed from the US soldiers who are living in the corridors of his Palace to protect his life.

After his homecoming, little is heard or seen of Aristide. He spends his days aimlessly, surrounded by his American bodyguards, in the suffocating Palace: the air-conditioning has been stolen too. There is no money for governing. And probably, once the plumber has been paid to reconnect the water, no money for new air-conditioning.

The hastily assembled American set is starting to wobble. In places it is threatening to collapse before the show has even begun. At the booted feet of a GI lies the body of a Haitian soldier, deposited as an offering by a grateful people.

'No, no, no! That's not what we do in a democracy! No, no, no, very bad!' yells the GI, in an effort to leap the language barrier between him and the lynch mob. To emphasize his point, he waves his forefinger reprovingly under their noses. They look up at him in adoration, their sticks still dripping with blood.

Most Haitians seem not to have grasped the fact that last week's 'Fad', Saddams and Fidels have become this week's allies in restoring democracy. Still assuming that the US has come to annihilate the Haitian army, the people are spontaneously offering to lend the Liberators a hand. In some places they have been storming barracks and ripping 'Fad' soldiers to pieces. In others the army has evaporated, as the Pentagon had predicted. The soldiers have taken off their uniforms and gone to ground. So the Americans are now frugal with what's left of the 'Fad': 'Fad' soldiers may not be ideal, but they are the only 'police' that Haiti has. Until the blue helmets arrive to create a new police force, the Americans must try to keep as many Haitian soldiers at their posts as they can.

The soldier at our feet is still just alive. As the Americans lift his crumpled body into the back of their truck, the victim gets a few more well-aimed coconuts thrown at his head.

'No, no, no! Cut that out!' the American screams at the crowd, angry now. He turns to me. 'Jesus, what animals! Where the hell is the goddamn UN to get us out of here?'

To prevent more bloodletting, the disarmed 'Fad' get their weapons back. FRAPH members were never disarmed.

### UN: 'America must disarm Haiti'

Port-au-Prince, 4 November 1994 – In a series of statements the UN has expressed its unease about the lack of security in Haiti. America, however, is not prepared to take any extra measures. 'We cannot disarm Haiti,' said a spokesman for President Clinton. 'There are too many weapons here.'

The US Army is due to be replaced by around 6,000 UN soldiers. Boutros-Ghali is rumoured to have said that he does not want to send any blue helmets to Haiti before their security can be guaranteed. 'The US does not want to stay and the UN does not want to come,' said an American diplomat.                                    (*New York Times*)

'Who are those men in the blue hats?' asks Maurice as he shuffles in for morning coffee at the Oloffson. Several UN military personnel sit filling in forms a few tables along. They are part of the group of seventeen observers whom the UN has sent to check whether the security of blue helmets in Haiti can yet be guaranteed.

'They are the United Nations,' I say. 'They are coming here for a year to help you maintain democracy.'

Maurice's brow furrows. 'United stations . . . united stations . . .' he experiments for a while, then gives up. 'No, never heard of them.'

'I'm dead. I died yesterday evening at eight o'clock precisely, age thirty-one, cause unknown.' Dan Brown, life insurance detective, giggles chubbily. The UN observer, an Irishman, throws him an uncertain glance. He and Brown flew into Port-au-Prince this morning on the same plane, Brown for the first time since the invasion, the Irishman for the first time in his life.

Brown taps his death certificate. 'Cost me ten dollars. That's cheap for conclusive evidence that Haitian documents are no kind of evidence at all.'

'Aha!' nods the UN soldier with interest. He pulls out a notebook and scribbles down something with a camouflaged ballpoint pen.

'The old died-abroad-trick,' explains Brown and proceeds to inform us that this official confirmation of his death will be added to the extensive collection of false papers on the wall of his New York office. He hands us his business card. It describes him as 'Private Eye'.

Brown loves to have us along and we set off hand-in-hand for the *cimetière*, the graveyard at the heart of Port-au-Prince. After that he plans to go on to the mortuary for a look in the freezers, cast-offs from American hospitals and rumoured to run at a constant boiling point. Dan Brown hunts down the world's living dead. He is brought in when relatives demand pay-outs on people whom the insurance company believes are still with us.

'Almost nobody dies within two years of taking out a policy. So we always find that suspicious. I visit the hometown of the alleged deceased, question the local authorities, chat to neighbours and to the gravediggers at the churchyard, that kind of thing.'

First Services, the New York detective bureau for whom Brown works, is used by more than 200 (mostly American) insurance companies and unleashed on an army of swindlers who are jointly responsible for losses amounting to several billion per year. Insurers are even more suspicious if a claim comes from a war zone or disaster area. New York saw an unprecedented peak in false claims during the Gulf War.

'There's cash in chaos,' says Brown. This impresses the UN observer. He makes another note.

Brown's range extends into every continent. He covers over sixty countries. 'As a boy I wanted to be Indiana Jones,' he says. To me he looks more like Hercule Poirot, if a bit more disarming. His plan is to do Haiti once every two months in future. 'By then I'll have built up another bag full of claims, 80 per cent of them false. And New York usually faxes another batch through.' His colleagues are only too pleased with Brown's penchant for regions associated with mosquitoes, impassable roads, disease and political violence.

It turns out that even Haitian bot pippel have had the foresight to insure themselves. The US Coastguard, who are still recovering large groups from the Caribbean and repatriating them to the restored democracy, estimate that half of all Haitian tubs capsize and sink on the way to Florida. Thousands of bot pippel per year could be drowning like this. Take the parents who heard that their two teenage sons had drowned. There was no proof of their fate, but witnesses had seen the boys boarding a vessel in Port-au-Prince.

'The insurance company wanted to take the case to court,' says Brown. 'Legally they were in a strong position: even if they were dead, the boys would have drowned as a result of committing a punishable offence, since it's illegal to make the voyage without an American visa. But I advised them to pay out. Any jury would have given the distraught parents the benefit of the doubt.

'I am a completely unexpected phenomenon,' he goes on chirpily. 'Who is going to figure on an American insurance detective descending on some shit-hole like Saint-Jean-des-Deux-Eglises-sur-Mer?'

All sorts of 'evidence' drops through Brown's letter box, presented in all kinds of forms: death-notices from local papers, heart-breaking eye-witness letters in airmail envelopes, home videos of funerals, the on-camera testimony of doctors, policemen and officials from the Registry of Births, Marriages and Deaths, all swearing that the deceased is indeed dead.

'You will not be surprised to hear that the absolute winner in our collection is a Haitian production,' says Brown. 'Video arrives, accompanied by a claim for $50,000 in favour of the widow. We look at the pictures of the funeral. Get dozens of sobbing family members filing past, broken with grief. Camera zooms in on coffin. We see the loved one, in his best suit, arms crossed over his chest. We take another look. And bingo! Beads of sweat on his upper lip.'

Claim rejected.

The gates of the municipal cemetery have been torn off and sold to one of Port-au-Prince's many scrap-metal dealers, as has every usable component of Papa Doc Duvalier's mausoleum. All the decorative wrought-ironwork commemorating the cruel dictator has been melted down and reused. All that remains of Duvalier's grave is a small compost heap covered with weeds.

The *cimetière* looks like a marshalling yard for dilapidated bathrooms. The tombs were originally tiled from top to bottom. I recognize a design from my toilet at home; a shiny-glazed tulip motif in soft pink and green. The compartments hold two or three bodies on top of each other. None of the tombs is intact. We follow Brown and a gravedigger, stumbling over the rubble, in search of the fresh grave of a policy-holder.

Tombstones come with burning black candles or coagulated wax stumps to exorcize spirits. The stench of rotting human flesh hangs between the family tombs: walls have been knocked in and coffins dragged out through the holes to be broken open. One of them stands upended against a purple-glazed ruin, revealing a half-decayed rib cage. Wreathes and photos of the dead lie about, trampled and forgotten. It is windless and scorching hot between the tightly clustered little buildings. The sound of our footsteps echoes from the high perimeter wall. A jawbone cracks under the soles of my flip-flops. The UN observer clears his throat. I hear him swallowing.

The dead are still keeping some Haitians alive, even after the restoration of democracy. The gravedigger points out the smouldering cooking fires. 'They live here, the scum,' he says and describes how they set to at night, with sledgehammers and crowbars. They sell the brass coffin handles back to the coffin makers, the grave clothes to second-hand clothing dealers. Gold teeth and the rings and watches worn by the dead can be easily disposed of. Intact skulls find a market with voodoo priests and the coffins themselves are dismantled plank by plank and hastily removed.

Relatives do what they can to fight back. Coffin handles are increasingly made of gold-painted plastic. Wreathes are now made of real flowers, which last barely an hour in this climate. The traditional metal wreathes are gone almost as soon as they are laid.

'This month I have already plugged thirteen thieves,' brags the boss of the cemetery, tapping his hip-pistol.

'No kidding,' nods Brown appreciatively. And to us: 'This havoc is as much the fault of the city authorities as anybody else. They rent out a plot and if the family falls behind with the rent, it's "get out of here". You're just dumped, coffin and all, on the path.' The UN soldier's hand feels for his notebook and pen.

The tombs are taller than a man. In places they are packed so close that we can no longer squeeze between them. Then, like every other visitor, we clamber up on top and jump from tombstone to tombstone. More municipal shortcomings soon become apparent. With every shower the groundwater rises. It sloshes in the coffins. A voodoo priest, swathed in white, brandishes a dildo to ward off demons. Feathers and blood, left over from earlier sacrifices, stick to the surrounding tiles.

'Good afternoon,' says Brown.

The priest waves the plastic penis in friendly reply.

Brown comes to this graveyard nearly every day. 'If the deceased is buried in an unmarked grave, I get different people to lead me there, to see if they all point out the same place. Sometimes they bring me to an empty hole. Then they say, "We buried him here, but he got up and walked away."' The popular zombie-trick. Even though zombies are outlawed by the Constitution. Article 249 forbids the use of substances which 'induce a lethargic coma indistinguishable from death'. Because when the voodoo priest administers the *coup poudre*, the powder curse, the victim falls into a coma. Heartbeat and breathing fall to a level so low that they cannot be registered. The victim is pronounced dead and then buried. But in the night following the solemnities the priest appears in the graveyard. He revives the 'body' with an antidote and the zombie rises from the grave, confused, disorientated and with no will of his own. He has lost his memory and suffers from hallucinations. Handing out the *coup poudre* is therefore regarded as murder, even when the victim survives.

'Was that Article 294?' asks the UN observer.

'249,' corrects Brown. 'But I can't base my findings on that. I operate under US law, which makes no allowance for zombies.'

When we find the grave Brown is looking for, the name fits. He compares the date of death with that given on the certificate. We look over his shoulder to help. By 'cause of death', the relatives have written 'Heart stopped'.

Occasionally a claim turns out to be legitimate. Then Brown can pay out. He remembers with intense pleasure being able to delight two children in a Haitian mountain hamlet with a quarter of a million dollars. Their parents had been killed in a car crash in Miami.

'Those kids lived with grandma, the pigs and the chickens in a hut made of palm leaves. They were so malnourished they had orange hair. I felt like the fairy in Cinderella.'

That evening we wave Brown goodbye. 'I'm off to India now. They can think up a few things out there. I've got a dossier here on an Indian who'd just taken out invalidity insurance. Then he suddenly loses both legs and claims half a million. I suspect he's sawn them off himself. If I have time, I'll do Nigeria on the way home. It's bingo there on every case.'

The porter lugging his dossiers urges him to keep moving. As Brown disappears behind the customs shed, the UN observer shakes his head as if already doubting whether Brown had ever existed at all.

'I think I'll turn in early this evening,' he says. 'Tomorrow will be a long day. There's even more to be done here than I feared.'

In the Carrefour neighbourhood we are caught in a classic

tropical shower. The rain buckets down. Port-au-Prince lies at the foot of high mountains and you don't need this much water to turn the streets into churning rivers, complete with rapids which bring all forms of traffic, American military patrols included, to a total standstill. With the hillsides stripped bare of their few remaining trees by Haitians desperate for firewood and boats to escape the embargo, the top soil washes straight off. The water is a brown ooze. We dare not go further because we can't see the bottom of the rivers. After years without maintenance the streets are full of deep potholes. We can't see the manholes either, whose covers have long ago been filched and sold. So we are obliged to wait out the rain under the canopy of a petrol station, which stands like an abandoned museum. All around us, people are taking showers under the drainpipes.

'What is it that the UN are coming to do precisely?' I ask the UN observer.

'Uphold democracy,' he replies. 'I am investigating whether there is any democracy to uphold. But first I have to find some blue paint for my helmet. New York Headquarters hasn't been able to fix us up with UN helmets yet.'

### American troops withdraw

Port-au-Prince, 24 January 1995 – The Aristide government believes that it is still too early for UN troops to replace the Americans. There are still 6,000 men left in Haiti from the original US invasion force of 20,000. In two months that number will have fallen to 3,000, who will comprise half the planned UN force of 6,000. UN troops will be under the command of an American general. Congress has expressed serious worries about the participation of American troops in the

UN force and point to the American dead in
Somalia. The main difference of opinion between
America and Haiti concerns the potential danger
of fugitive Haitian soldiers reorganizing themselves
after the US departure. Rising crime figures in
Haiti are being partially ascribed to these soldiers.
The Americans claim that they reflect 'ordinary
criminality'. 'There is less crime here than in any
city I've ever been to. You can't expect Nirvana
from one day to the next. It is time for us to leave,'
said an American spokesman.    (*Washington Post*)

There are seventeen UN observers. Military personnel
from New Zealand, France, Ireland, Bangladesh, Pakistan,
Argentina and Djibouti. They have moved into an MRE
boarding house in Pétionville, opposite the casino. A local
family has immediately taken up residence on a plastic shopping bag, right in front of their door.

'Somalia Revisited,' is the sombre comment of one New
Zealand major, a Maori. 'No sign of democracy here. Not a
trace. Anywhere. And there is no electricity, so we can't fax
Boutros-Ghali and tell him.'

In '*le pays en dehors*' (as the country is called in the town)
Haiti has more than 5,000 villages and rural settlements. Most
of them have never seen an American, either before the
invasion or after it. The invasion force, nearly all of which has
now been withdrawn from Haiti, never ventured beyond the
capital 'Pap' and the northern town of Cap-Haitien. The
provinces, home to 75 per cent of the population, were allo-
cated to a mere hundred men from Special Forces. Whether
this handful of elite troops could even have planted the seed of
democracy out there, let alone restored it, is open to question.
But the Americans claim that this is indeed the case.

Since they despatched Special Forces to the interior it has been quiet. 'Suspiciously quiet, we think,' says the UN Maori. 'The Americans claim that no news is good news, but we are going to follow the Forces trail to see if they really have established democratic order.'

The UN and the US have a serious difference of opinion over the definition of the term 'democratic order'. Just this morning the body of the Mayor of Hinche was found dumped in a ditch. Hinche is one of the 5,000-odd villages where Special Forces are in charge. The Maori has been asking around. 'One of their soldiers said to me, "Man, I come from Los Angeles. When you go out the door in the morning, you never know if you're gonna make it home alive in the evening. Compared with home, Haiti is safe and stable as hell." OK, the UN should not make a big fuss about a murder. You get murders in the healthiest democracies. But when the victim is a left-wing mayor whose head has been hacked off, then you can't blame me if I report it to Boutros-Ghali as a possible indication of continuing political instability.'

Haiti has the Secretary-General's full attention now that the operation in Rwanda is back on the rails, or so the Maori believes.

'What does he do with your reports?' I ask.

'I don't know. Complain about them to Clinton maybe? At least that's what we hope.'

Special Forces in northern Haiti are commanded by Captain Max, a man whose reputation has gone a long way before him. They say he has conquered the whole province virtually alone. Now he is based in the most inaccessible part of the country, in a town called Port-de-Paix. According to rumour, he rules with an iron hand, like an absolute prince, cold-blooded and cruel. His subjects have to go to bed at seven o'clock in the evening, on pain of death. Or so I've heard.

The UN observers – an Irish major and his colleague from Djibouti – whose portfolio includes Max's kingdom, have already met Max face to face. 'He's just like a Teenage Mutant Ninja Turtle,' says the Irishman. 'And soon he'll be replaced by blue helmets who won't have even a rolling pin to wave. After the show that Max has put on, the question is whether the local population will take us impotent missionaries seriously.'

He seems to think that I should meet Max, because Max is to be relieved by a UN team of Dutch military police and Belgian gendarmes. Their job will be to set up a new police force in Port-de-Paix. There are no telephone links and radio contact is intermittent. Once or twice a month an American ship brings in petrol and supplies, weather permitting.

Anyone who wants to see Max in person has to go to his kingdom. It's a long slog to get there, as it turns out. The rainy season has not even begun and already each shower is eroding the verges of the sole road to Port-de-Paix. I nestle down on the back seat of the white UN Land Rover. It won't be long before the only way to reach Max's kingdom will be by mule.

Loose stones crunch under our slow-moving wheels and the bodywork bangs against every bump in the road. With some difficulty we pass trucks making even slower progress than we are. They are so overloaded with people and goods that the only place left for the livestock is on the outside. The goats are trussed together upside down. One goat's head is so close to the ground that the creature has to brace its neck back to avoid being dashed to pieces.

'Emenems, Emenems!' scream the small children as we drive through a village. Captain Max and his men must have recently passed by distributing American sweets.

'Don't drive so fast, or you'll have us in the ravine,' the Djiboutian is saying yet again.

'I'm not driving fast. You always drive just as fast,' replies the Irishman. The UN observers sit in the front like a bickering couple. They have been paired for only three weeks and are already getting on each other's nerves. The Irishman points to the pigs wallowing in the mud at the side of the road. 'Mmmm, look at those delicious piggies, Mohammed. Fancy lunch?' he says.

'Yuk! Can't you stop going on about that?'

'You never hear me complaining about you wanting to pray five times a day.'

To prevent reports arriving in New York tainted by nationality, UN teams are as mixed as possible. In practice this means a constant search for compromise on what gets reported. The Irishman sees Haiti as Ireland, where a potato famine cost more than a million Irish lives and drove a million more to flee the country. It happened over 150 years ago, but Irish children are still raised with the fear of hunger. 'Nobody understands people having to flee to escape starvation like we do,' says the Irishman. 'That's why Ireland is always the first to support UN humanitarian actions.'

To Djibouti's Mohammed, Haiti looks very different. He too is reminded of his own country. He loves Djibouti and serves it faithfully, but he has always imagined Paradise as looking very like Haiti: i.e. wet. He scarcely notices the people past whom we are splashing, he sees only the rain. 'Haiti is blessed,' he enthuses to me over his shoulder. All blessings come from above in Djibouti. In this case, literally. 'How we'd love to have such muddy roads in Djibouti.' So refugees who choose America over this Garden of Eden are to him incomprehensible. Why the Americans, and then the UN, should have to go to such trouble to keep the Haitians at home is a mystery to him: such a muddy country can't have any real problems.

The mandate of UN observers is to observe. Every destitute roadside Haitian is therefore observed and driven past, with a friendly wave. 'That's the least we can do. They've had UN vehicles driving through their villages for weeks. We prefer not to stop, because we'd be immediately mobbed by people begging for things that we can't provide. A lift, because the tap-tap they were in has slid off the road and they've got to get home. Medicines. A job with Brown & Root, who are virtually the only employer in Haiti at the moment. It wears you down, having to say No all the time.'

Almost no villager responds to our greeting. People look up bored as we pass them, or point at their empty bellies in reproach.

'That means they are hungry,' I say.

'I know, I know. Don't rub it in,' growls the Irishman.

We bounce through settlements of barely a dozen huts. Dead chickens hang from the doorposts. The heads have been ripped from the bodies: offerings to the voodoo spirits. 'You can't blame them. I bet the gods can do more for these people than the UN can,' says the Irishman.

We slither on two wheels past a deep ravine. The Irishman nudges Mohammed and points to the half-naked women who are washing themselves in the river below. 'You probably think they should be stoned, don't you?'

'Not at all. They are savages who don't know any better and so we can spare them,' his colleague replies with irritation.

After yet another mountain pass, the road drops down towards the sea. And still wrangling, we finally enter Port-de-Paix.

The walls of the town are decorated with paintings that show attachés being exterminated by jets of flames spewed from mysterious sticks. The sticks are being wielded by creatures that look a bit like the daleks in *Dr Who*. But there is no mistaking US Special Forces in full combat gear. The Port-de-Paix streets are unpaved. The citizens, barefoot and resigned, wade through the knee-deep mud in the rain. In the middle of town rises a dripping crag, on top of which stands a massive fort, left behind by the French slave masters. I stare up at the crows circling in the dark sky above it.

'*Le château de Capitain Max*,' says a passer-by proudly.

Mohammed sets off for the only hotel in town. 'I've seen enough of him. I'll leave him to you two.'

The Irishman and I take a deep breath and slowly begin to climb the winding path. The rain buckets down from the sky.

A windy parking area. 'Quartier Général du Département Militaire du Nord-Ouest' is engraved above the gate of the fort. There has never been any maintenance: rusting steel reinforcing rods protrude from holes in the concrete walls and in the broad steps. The mustard yellow paint is mildewed and peeling, and the cannons on both sides of the steps are lost under the weight of overgrown rhododendrons. American APCs, jeeps, trailer bikes and horses are parked in pairs at the foot of the steps. The dripping horses tear up the long grass with their great yellow teeth. Max and his men only patrol in their APCs where the winding tracks are wide enough, but the Haitians are no longer surprised to see *les Américains* on horseback, or racing past on their motor bikes. And as the rainy season progresses, they'll get used to seeing groups of Ninja Turtles negotiating the rapids in rubber boats.

We climb a wooden ladder to the roof of the fort. From there we can survey the entire North-west: the town, the valley in which it stands, the broad river we had to cross to get here and the surrounding mountains. And right in front of us, the sea. In the little harbour, a few half-sunken fishing boats and some collapsed jetties. A small sloop, the *Misère Malheureux*, is approaching with a pile of coconuts on board. The crew have to bail and row at the same time.

'I rule by fear. Anyone who doesn't co-operate, I shoot.' We turn and see Max gazing out over his kingdom, bared chest thrust out like a shield in the downpour. No sign of the goose bumps.

'So, the UN have come back to see if I'm still doing my job properly . . .'

The Captain is certainly impressive. His dark eyes are sunk deep in their sockets and his head is shaved bald. An automatic weapon dangles from his square shoulders. A pistol is strapped to one muscled thigh, a long jungle knife to the other. He must go through life armed to the teeth. The Irishman takes me by a wet arm and thrusts me forward.

'She comes from Holland,' he says quickly.

'Ah, DutchBat!' Max smiles benignly. 'How nice to see you. It is so awfully stable and safe here, I was beginning to get bored. Now come, my dear. Let me introduce you to my men.'

One of the halls in the fort has been set up as an operations room. On the TV, CNN is reporting on murder and death in Rwandan refugee camps. 'While Jews are remembering the genocide inflicted on them fifty years ago, the UN can find no solution for Rwanda,' the Rwandan Ambassador to the UN is indignantly telling a reporter. 'It was unable to stop the genocide of Rwandan Tutsis and is now failing to ensure the arrest of mass murderers who have fled to the camps.'

The interview is half drowned by crackling radios, as they strive to establish contact with US Army Headquarters in Port-au-Prince. Unmade camp beds are strewn with maps, helmets and automatic weapons. I take in Max's men. With scarves knotted round shaven heads, rifles and pistols dangling nonchalantly around legs and muddied leather boots under dirty camouflage uniforms, they look just like pirates. Some are asleep in their hammocks. Hair bristles through open shirts. A couple are cleaning their nails with notched jungle knives. Others are cursing their way through a poker game.

The Irishman looks round the scattered equipment with envy: since his arrival in Haiti he has been filling in endless forms to get a blue helmet. The only thing that currently identifies him as a UN soldier is a blue headscarf, tucked fussily into the breast-pocket of his national uniform. It actually belongs to his wife who, well acquainted with the UN, had popped it into his suitcase just before he left for Haiti.

'Hey guys, DutchBat is here,' yells Max over the din.

'Well ain't that nice,' drawls a Special Force lazily.

The only running water in Port-de-Paix flows right down Main Street, abundantly after each shower. I have just rinsed the thickest deposits of mud from my calves, using a bucket of water brought by somebody from the hotel. So I'm ready for a night on the town.

Captain Max drives up in his Humvee, a small private tank, and gallantly opens the door. A machine gun is welded between the two rear seats. The barrel extends threateningly forward between us. We rumble through the streets.

'Smile and wave, smile and wave.' It sounds like an order. Max's large hand goes routinely back and forth. We wave to the market women who are spattered with mud from our broad tyres, throw kisses to wet little kids and lean out to shake both the hands of a skinny old man in a wheelchair. He is stranded in the middle of the road, surrounded by brown water.

'The village plumber,' says Max as we move on. 'He is pushed up the hill to my fort every morning to offer his

services, by his grandson.' But Special Forces can do everything for themselves, says Max. And on we drive through the
mud to our dinner date, waving all the while like a stand-in
Bill and Hillary.

The Bien Venue is the only restaurant in Port-de-Paix to
have survived three years of embargo. They have a chicken,
but she is still hopping around in the courtyard, so it could
take a while.

Rambo was a US Army Special Force too. Sewed his own
flapping flesh straight back on to his biceps without a flinch.
Went and did the Vietnam War all over again on his own and
won because that was his mission. 'Is *Rambo* like it is in real
life?' I ask Max.

Surprised at this stupid question, Max nods seriously. 'We're
the best troops of the best army in the world. It would
be sooooooo dumb for anyone to try and fight us.' These
super-knights errant operate without fear or reproach, prefer-
ably behind enemy lines, in small but sophisticated teams:
'Two pieces of rope, a Coca-Cola can and eight minutes is all
a Special Force needs to win a war,' runs the legend. Which
is not, according to Max, too far from the truth. 'Wherever
you put in a Special Force – in Iraq, Vietnam, El Salvador or
Haiti – he always emerges triumphant.'

A week after the invasion, small groups of Forces were put
down by helicopter amongst the goats and the chickens and
lopsided mud huts of a score of windy villages and townships,
the dumbfounded Haitians looking on. The fact that the
Americans had invaded Haiti had entirely escaped most of the
province's inhabitants. In villages with television there was no
electricity and in towns where people could have read about
it there were no newspapers. For some Haitians, the giant
*blancs* who leapt out of the swirling dust were the first they
had seen in their lives.

The conquest of the North-west took Max and his nine men about thirty seconds: the lion's share of local authority, soldiers and mayors included, had fled at the first rumour of the helicopters. Any local soldiers encountered were informed by Max that they must surrender immediately, and they, without a moment's hesitation, obeyed.

'"Look," I said. "I've come here to restore democracy. I will shoot anyone who doesn't co-operate. We are the Special Forces. Don't fuck with us. Do – not – fuck – with – us! Ever!"'

Only one Haitian officer had dared lodge a protest. 'He felt humiliated because he'd had to surrender to a nine-man team. I told him, "Nine of us are more than enough to send you all to hell." Since then, not a moment's trouble. They don't bother us. We don't bother them.'

I ask whether any Haitian authorities are left for DutchBat, soon to arrive with their UN colleagues from Belgium, to work with.

'There are still some soldiers, but I don't know what you could do with them. They hang around my fort. Don't dare go out on the street without us. Sometimes a group disappears off to Port-au-Prince. It seems like they have to take some six-day crash course in human rights. A lot of them never come back. Suits me, because I have to keep what's left of the Port-de-Paix garrison alive from my own rations. Nobody else does it.'

Quite apart from soldiers who don't want to work any more, Restore Democracy has a police force about whom serious doubts have arisen before they are even trained. Both the Haitian government and the UN have complained that, in their haste, the Americans are barely screening candidates for the police. Immediately after the invasion, recruitment posters were pasted to walls and trees throughout Haiti saying:

'Are you over twenty-five and healthy? Become a policeman.' This open invitation quickly attracted tens of thousands of unemployed, who had to be driven from the recruiting offices with tear gas. After all, these were the first job vacancies in Haiti for three years. While interviews are still dragging on, a team of American cops and Canadian Mounties have been hired to provide rapid professional training in improvised school buildings. There is no time to repeat anything in Operation Restore Democracy, so everyone graduates from the Police Academy.

'The UN will have to train them up on the job, but if you want to know the details, don't come to me. Go to Boutros Boutros Boutros. Or is it Ghali Ghali Ghali? And whether or not they succeed in making good policemen out of them makes no difference to us. We don't need them. Special Forces don't need anyone.'

'Yes, but our UN boys soon will,' I protest.

'What for? Nothing ever happens here,' says Max.

With the Haitian army mostly on the run and a new police force still being trained, North-west Haiti has no government at all. But for as long as Max is here, it has no crime either.

'Nobody dares to do anything wrong with me around,' says Max. 'Criminality in the whole province is zero. At least, no complaints have reached us.' There have been a few from the town, but Max is not interested.

'People come to me regularly to complain about the captain of a refugee boat. "He accepted money to take me to Miami and then didn't show up," they say. So I say, "OK, I'll grab this captain by the balls for you, but then I'll arrest you too, because you're not allowed to go to Miami." They don't hang around.'

I ask whether Max has searched his kingdom for weapons belonging to the attachés. He gives me a quizzical look. 'No chance of disarming them. Most villages will be inaccessible until the dry season. The roads are washed away and we haven't enough horses and motor bikes to get through. And even if we could, we'd have to search the houses. Combing through thousands of houses and huts, tens of thousands maybe, with nine men. And every hut you go into looks like *Steptoe and Son*. Get real!'

'So you're going to leave the dirty work to our boys, then?'

'Yup, sure looks like it,' replies Max.

I'll have to report this to my UN travelling companions: the Irishman and the Djiboutian could not be here this evening. Max's orders.

'Smile and wave, smile and wave.' We have dined, and are now back in Max's tank waving, as we plough through the muddy evening streets en route for the studio of La Voix du Nord-Ouest. People are hurrying home. There is still just time: in fifteen minutes begins both the curfew that Max has imposed and the talk-show he hosts on the radio. After landing in Port-de-Paix he immediately confiscated and repaired the local radio station, and now broadcasts live several evenings a week.

We sit propped in a sound-proof cubicle, with old carpet nailed to the wall to improve the acoustics. Posters pinned to the carpet announce performances by popular Haitian bands: Les Fantômes, who were apparently to be heard in May three years ago at a Port-au-Prince club, and Sweet Mickey, who emigrated to the States after the coup against Aristide and never came back. Two microphones are live: one for the muddy-booted translator who squats beside Max, one for Max himself.

'Good eeeeeeeevening Port-de-Paix!!!' roars Max to begin the programme. The sound metres register red.

'*Bonsoir, Port-de-Paix,*' comes the calm translation.

'You've behaved yourselves this week. For that I love you to death! Maybe, just maybe, I'll put the curfew back an hour next week. But for now . . . what's been happening in our beautiful Port-de-Paix since we arrived? As you know, we've been here since September 27.'

'*Nous sommes ici depuis septembre vingt-sept . . .*'

'We're proud and happy to be here . . .'

'*Nous sommes fiers et heureux d'être ici . . .*'

'Since we've been here, you've seen four ships come in with supplies. There is food. There is petrol. We have electricity for a few hours every day and all day Sunday. And all this is thanks to *les Américains*, don't you forget that. Today I am proud to announce that the telephone at the post office is working again. And now: music!' The red light on Max's mike goes out. 'French elevator music,' he says dismissively.

The impact of his radio talks is enormous, says Max. 'For example, two weeks ago I told the listeners, "The rainy season is almost upon us, so I want you all to get rid of the trash in the gutters in front of your houses, so that we don't get any blockages and floods." The next day I see hundreds of them, no thousands, hard at it with brooms. So I'm happy, till I see that everyone's dumping their trash in the neighbour's gutter. The UN will have do something quick about community spirit in this town.' The final notes of Haitian muzak are dying away.

'Come on, you're on next,' commands Max.

'*Bonsoir, Port-de-Paix,*' I rasp. 'I come from Holland and I'm here to see how the Americans are doing . . . [Max glares at me] . . . and they are doing *fantastique!*'

Every morning a small crowd still gathers in front of the fort, in the firm conviction that Max will have finally disposed of the 'Fad' soldiers during the night. When the first one comes out with a towel round his waist and a toothbrush, resentful booing rises from the tense ranks. By the time the third soldier appears, very alive, people drift away disappointed.

I find Max on the steps. He is supervising a group of puffing local soldiers as they do push-ups. Astonished children stare from the bushes. 'Everything just as safe and under control as yesterday and tomorrow,' he says. Some piglets are pushing their noses into his crotch. He idly pushes them away with his M-16.

Reminders of the policy of absenteeism fostered by the ousted military regime hang on the fort's walls. Yellowed instructions relate to attendance lists. Since the arrival of Max and his men, most of the old guard have still not turned up to work. Those who have come are refugees from other parts of Haiti, seeking his protection. The fort has become a sort of asylum centre for soldiers hiding from the revenge of the populace. There are forty-eight of them at the moment. Max has made them count themselves.

In the courtyard I come across the entire military band from Cap-Haitien. They have abandoned their drums and tubas and fled here, 100 kilometres away. After a four-day trek across rough country, they have finally found Max and thrown themselves upon his protection. He has allowed them to stay. The disbanded band now sits behind dented pans in front of a dark shed. Making music, I assume, but as I get closer I see that they're cooking a meal.

'I played the trumpet,' says one of them sadly.

'And I was the conductor,' says another. A rat trots past behind him. These soldiers are in civvies. Whether they will soon become keen cadets for the UN police corps, I rather doubt. 'We left our uniforms at home so that we wouldn't be recognized as soldiers,' says the conductor. He cracks his fingers nervously. 'We have no idea if we can still work. We're waiting for orders, but now that our general is in Panama we don't know who we should get them from. People say that we will be punished for the coup against Aristide and maybe for other coups too. But we don't know anything about them. We just played music in Cap-Haitien and we've never even seen a president in the flesh. Captain Max says that we must wait to see what democracy has in store for us. For the moment we're just keeping safe inside here.'

Max shows me the Haitian soldiers' sleeping quarters. There are no mattresses on the bunks. Never have been, according to Max. The sodden wooden floor, with its wide cracks between the boards, makes a lethal impression. There are no windows and no bulbs in the light-fittings. The toilet bowls are cracked and full of excrement.

'Worse than a slum, isn't it? And this was where the authorities lived! What's the name of that dude who was the boss? Cédras? Generaaaal Cédras even. Well, since we've been here he is definitely passé, let me assure you. Never hear his name any more. No wonder, when you see how his people were forced to exist.'

A timid knock on the wooden door of Max's operations room: a Haitian officer looks hesitantly round the corner.

'Welcome, brother,' says Max graciously. The Haitian looks grateful. Max turns to me.

'This is *mon colonel* Clerjeune, just appointed governor of the North-west on my orders. His predecessor has vanished. "I have to go off for a moment, but I'll be back tomorrow," he said the morning after we landed. I've never seen him since.'

Clerjeune looks like an amiable schoolmaster with thick

spectacles on a friendly round head. But I know better. In reality he is a monster, one of the Port-au-Prince military mafia. Clerjeune was once head of the 'Anti-Gang' department, which ostensibly hunted down major criminals, but in fact ran torture chambers into which the enemies of the regime disappeared. It was Clerjeune who personally tortured Aristide's Mayor of Port-au-Prince with lighted cigarettes. After three years in hiding, his victim has just returned to his desk in City Hall, where he is surrounded by dozens of American soldiers. The attack-prevention service.

'Isn't it amazing?' Max throws an arm around Clerjeune and gives him a firm squeeze. '*Mon colonel* and I both went to the same school. We were both educated at Fort Benning, USA. He speaks American. Try him.'

'You must be very pleased with the American invasion,' I say.

'I have received orders to work with the Americans and I am acting on those orders,' he mutters. He sneaks a quick glance at Max, who nods in satisfaction.

Port-au-Prince comes through on the radio and Max is called to the microphone. Clerjeune uses the opportunity to continue our conversation in French. Max and his elite troops speak Russian, Japanese and Arabic, but no French.

'*Les Américains* say that they're going home soon. That United Nations soldiers are coming to take their place. Blue helmets!' Clerjeune's expression implies something grubby.

'The international community can't do that to us, leave us here with only blue helmets to protect us. They are useless. If we are to survive we need more Captain Maxes, as many of them as possible.' Clerjeune shudders.

'I reckon you're right,' I say. 'What a dreadful prospect for you.'

Max, his radio conversation at an end, slings his ammunition belt across his chest and climbs into his Humvee. 'Just off to arrest the school principal,' he explains and tears off down the hill.

The few remaining teachers in Port-de-Paix have threatened to go on strike. They have not been paid for three years. The suspicion is that the principal has been pocketing the incoming salaries.

'Strikes threaten stability. That's why I took an interest,' says Max later. 'I poked my M-16 into the principal's fat belly and said: "I am arresting you for illegally breathing." I would have done too, but he immediately came up with the overdue pay-packets.'

'Don't say you're impressed by that big-mouth, Lin?' the Irishman asks as we drive out of Port-de-Paix.

I am. Deeply. To Captain Max a kingdom, to the blue helmets not even a blue helmet.

'Weeeell,' I say, 'maybe a bit.'

'Because no doubt it's all very clever for nine guys to get a whole district under their thumb,' he goes on, 'but people tend to co-operate if you put a machine gun to their heads. We could do it too, couldn't we, Mohammed, if they let us get on with it. But we're never allowed to do anything. A bit of observing, that's all we get. A chance to watch The Amazing Captain Max and his Special Forces show.'

The Irishman is still grumbling as we carefully nose the Land Rover into the wild river. The bridge was washed away in the last downpour. Halfway across we hear the drone of trailer bikes and are soon overtaken by Special Forces, yelling 'Yiii Haaa!' and soaking us from top to toe. The Irishman turns on the wipers and gazes after them with longing.

'Hey Mohammed, I've been thinking . . . if it keeps raining and the roads get even worse, we'll not be able to get through by car any more. Reckon the Security Council would give us some motor bikes too?'

'Not in a million years. They'd just say they couldn't afford it, as usual,' says the Djiboutian.

### UN troops take over Haiti from the Americans

New York, 20 January 1995 – The Security Council today commissioned Boutros-Ghali to mobilize 6,000 blue helmets for a peace mission in Haiti. The blue helmets will have to take over the positions of the US invasion force which forced the Haitian military regime to step down four months ago. The US Ambassador to the UN, Madeleine Albright, announced that the American army had completed its task in Haiti. 'This Security Council decision is an outstanding example of the way in which the UN can work with an army of intervention. The United States can now share the burden of Haiti.'

(UPI)

Boutros-Ghali already has half of his 6,000 blue helmets; he's been told to add 3,000 American soldiers to the UN payroll. Pakistan, Bangladesh and Nepal will provide the bulk of the remainder.

When I return to Port-de-Paix a few weeks later, the UN police-trainers from Holland and Belgium have safely arrived. This evening the respective commanders of the Dutch military police and the Belgian gendarmes are guests on La Voix du Nord-Ouest. By the time they have found the studio, Max is already on air. They stand in a stifling corridor, waiting for Max to summon them.

'After this little melody I'm going to introduce you to the newest guys on the block. Stay tuned, Port-de-Paix,' we hear through the intercom.

Muzak. Max beckons me into his cubicle first.

'What do you think of them, Lin? All grown-up men and they still want Special Forces to babysit them for a few weeks. They are scared to stay here on their own. Fairies!' He spits in the waste-paper bin. 'You won't hear me complaining again, so don't worry, but these jerks have been here a week now and done virtually nothing except fix up their hotel. By the time we'd been here a week we'd laid a new airstrip and delivered half a dozen babies by caesarean section. The people are already muttering. They know instinctively that the new *blancs* aren't as good as us. That's just too bad for them, because they'll all have to get along. But OK, I'm not such a bastard that I won't talk up the UN to the locals this evening. I used to recruit for the army, so I can sell ice-cubes to the Eskimos and telescopes to the blind if I have to. Selling the UN to the Haitians has got to be possible.'

Back in the programme, Max sets up a pounding bass.

'You'll have seen new faces in the street. New *blancs*, very nice guys, who have come to help set up the new police force. The policemen aren't there yet, but they soon will be. From now on, you'll be seeing fewer Americans around. But we'll be here in the background, so you don't have to be scared.'

I glance sideways. The two UN faces are frozen in horror. The Belgian is the first to thaw and creeps in behind the microphone. He says something about looking forward to a pleasant collaboration with the new police force, when it comes. Then the Dutchman pulls up a chair.

'Holland is a small country to the north of Belgium,' he begins. 'You all know Ruud Gullit and Marco van Basten.

We don't speak French as well as the Belgians. I have nothing
more to say now. Thank you.'

'And remember,' Max smoothly comes in, 'smile and wave.
Although they may not be Americans, smile and wave. We
cut away to a song now . . .'

'Cowboy,' says the Belgian, back in the corridor.

'Show-off,' agrees the Dutchman.


## II

America's Restore Democracy has now become the UN's
Uphold Democracy:

> ### Congress votes for limiting role in UN
>
> Washington, 17 February 1995 – The House of
> Representatives has passed a bill designed to drasti-
> cally limit the role of the United States in UN
> missions. The passage of the bill has been followed
> with increasing concern at UN Head Office in
> New York. Californian Congressman Rohrbacher
> summed up the views of the majority: 'After carry-
> ing the burden of world peace for forty years, it is
> time for America to give priority to her own inter-
> ests. America comes first.' The debate on the new
> law was a long litany of complaint against the UN.
> After the vote there were cheers and applause.
> 'This is a first step to ensure that in the future not
> a single American soldier will be forced to wear a
> blue beret and risk his life in countries where no
> American interests are involved,' said Republican
> Congressman Seastrand. The new law states that
> in principle American troops can no longer be

deployed under UN command, arguing that US armed forces are too well trained and equipped to serve under non-American command. It is also proposed to reduce the US contribution from 31.7 to 25 per cent of the UN budget. Further, the cost of American actions such as those in Somalia and Haiti should be deducted from American contributions to blue helmet missions.

Republican presidential candidate Dole also regards the UN as a discredited, badly led, superfluous, wasteful and, for American soldiers, dangerous organization.                    (*de Volkskrant*)

'You have to go to the UN for everything now, not to us any more.' The desk sergeant of the Civilian Affairs battalion smiles at the queue of civilians who think that they need the US Army for something.

'My chicken is dead,' repeats the old lady at the front of the queue. She lives high up on the cloud-topped mountain that rises from the centre of Cap-Haitien, and has come down today with a handful of bloody feathers. All that remains of her chicken after a collision with a tank. She has come to Base Port to seek redress from the Americans, because it was a *blanc* who ran over the bird.

'The US Army feels for you, ma'am, but you really should go to the UN. Les Nations Unies,' the soldier explains yet again, and then turning to me, 'It's not so difficult really, is it? Or is it?'

'A new chicken costs twenty-five gourdes,' says the old lady, stubbornly.

'The US Army will do you a favour, ma'am. I will write your complaint on a piece of paper, put a real American stamp on it and you can take it down to les Nations Unies. There

are a few of them up at the Montjoli Hotel, I believe. They'll
sort it out for you.'

'Isn't it easier to give her the twenty-five gourdes, then she
can get home before dark with her new chicken?' I suggest.
'It's only a couple of dollars.'

'No way,' says the sergeant. 'The news would spread like
wildfire: *les Américains* are giving money away. We'd have the
whole of Haiti on the doorstep next morning! And it's got
nothing to do with us any more.'

Cap-Haitien too has a new police force in training. It doesn't
look very promising, even though its American and Canadian
trainers are doing their best to create that impression. On the
wall, in an almost heart-breaking attempt to build up good
PR, hang pamphlets which say: 'Feel free to call us. We are
at your service 24 hours a day.' An invitation from the brand
new police force. I call the telephone number immediately,
of course, and get the out-of-order tone.

Police cadets have to be accompanied on the street by UN
police trainers. One such, a Canadian, courteously opens the
door of his white jeep. A murder suspect is sitting on the back
seat, his hands tied behind his back, helpless.

'There are quite a few potholes in the road and he can't
hold on to anything. If he looks like falling over, do me a
favour and see that he doesn't bang anything with his teeth,'
says the Canadian. Two members of the new police force
should really have come along this morning to take care of
the murderer, but they haven't shown up. 'You can never
find them when there's work to be done. And certainly not if
it's about following the correct legal procedures in murder
cases. My pupils would rather shoot murder suspects straight
off, to get rid of them. They regard a trial as a waste of scarce
resources.'

Today the suspect has to be brought before the court. The nearest judge to have stayed at his post in spite of the invasion lives 75 kilometres away.

'It's going to cost us a whole day to get there, but someone in this country has to show some respect for the law. If it isn't the police, it'll just have to be the blue helmets,' says the Canadian, waving to Haitians at the roadside. One of them points to his belly and sticks up his middle finger as we drive past. An international gesture, even in the Haitian interior it seems.

It is the hottest hour of the day when we pull up on the trampled earth in the centre of a village. There is a wooden church and a tree, the only one in sight. Wind like the air from a hairdryer blows clouds of dust from the bare landscape straight through the village. A short distance away are a couple of huts made of dried mud. A horse is tethered to a post at the side of the road. It looks at us. Apart from the horse and a lonely pig snuffling around, the place appears deserted. The track which has brought us over the Plain du Nord runs past the tree and away towards the hills of the even more desolate Plateau du Nord.

A wooden board, fixed to the gable of one of the huts, hangs slanting in the wind. Upon it is written 'Justice de la Paix'. Corrugated iron roof. No doors. I peer inside: cobwebs on wooden beams.

There is movement on the far side of the square. An old man is being carried out of a hut by two younger men. The judge. He is bent and shrunk with age. His black pinstripe suit is far too big, clearly a relic of younger days. His sockless feet poke into shoes with loose flapping soles. On his head, a straw hat.

The judge has only one arm. He drapes his empty sleeve over the little table as he is helped on to his chair inside the hut. The two porters remain standing behind him. On the wall above their heads, a crucifix. The crucified hangs with his feet on a skull.

The villagers know immediately that there's something to see and a handful of them peer through the open windows with interest. The judge has laid aside the pile of papers handed over by the Canadian. He hasn't read them. He doesn't have his glasses with him. The defendant stands before him, head bowed in submission.

'What's his name?' asks the old judge to nobody in particular. His only teeth are on the right side of his mouth.

'Lorelus,' replies the Canadian.

'What?'

'Lorelus!' chorus the audience helpfully.

'Who?'

'LORELUS!' screams everybody.

'Guilty,' says the judge and rises from his chair.

The Canadian and I stare after the judge in utter bewilderment as he is carried back to the hut on the other side of the square.

'So on we go then,' says the Canadian finally. 'The O. J. Simpson trial has its critics too.' He helps the condemned man back into the jeep. I slide in beside him and wedge him as tight as I can.

When the last US soldiers based at the harbour of Port-au-Prince were withdrawn and sent to Kuwait (Saddam's army was on a manoeuvre), Brown & Root, with 769 of its own people and 1,047 Haitian employees, assumed control of the port until further notice. Thus it was that Lieutenant-Colonel McManus, US Army (retired), who had earned his stripes in Vietnam's Cam Ranh Bay, became Haiti's new harbour master.

'The Haitians are lucky to get us. Thanks to Brown & Root, ships are unloaded in half the time and nobody has to pay bribes any more,' he says.

Indeed two potential foreign investors are coming to look at the promising new handling methods in use at the harbour. They don't yet know that it won't last long. Brown & Root are not planning to stay on in Haiti without the US army.

The two entrepreneurs come from the neighbouring Turks and Caicos Islands. Lured by the great lambi shells found on the local seabed, they are thinking of setting up a little shell-processing factory. They know from experience that these shells go down well in the US, where they use them as ashtrays.

'Do you happen to know where we could find a mayor or someone like that, with whom we could go over investment conditions? We've been to the US Embassy, but they told us to go to the UN. The UN said that Haiti has a government and that we should apply to them. The government has no telephone, or it has a telephone but doesn't answer it, or it answers and says it knows nothing about it.'

I think I might be able to help them. It is a national holiday and I do indeed know where the Mayor of Port-au-Prince will be hanging out today. I take the potential investors with me to the Champs de Mars.

Blue helmets from Bangladesh are stationed on the city's smoggy intersections, to try and keep the honking lines of cars and tap-taps moving. Petrol is now flowing freely. Street kids, high from sniffing glue, in oversized trousers and T-shirts, with orange hair on heads aged by hunger, hang round the UN soldiers' legs. They last ate the day before yesterday and know that you can sometimes scrounge something from blue helmets.

The air is saturated with moisture and it is 40° Celsius when a band sets up on an improvised stage. The Mayor appears with a guitar under his arm. He launches into an anti-imperialist number, the drums drowning the guitar. 'I am a Marxist,' he says into the microphone between verses.

The two investors have seen enough. 'They have exactly the same shells in the Dominican Republic,' they say, as they bid me farewell and head for the airport.

The Mayor was elected last week in Haiti's first local elections since democracy was restored. Aristide's endorsement was sufficient: Manno Charlemagne, Haiti's king of the soft protest song, swept into City Hall with 45 per cent of the vote. Several times a day he rises from Room 20 at the Hotel Oloffson and crosses the veranda to the fax machine, strumming an imaginary guitar as he goes. He is disappointed every time: there is still no message from Bob Dylan. Manno is trying to correspond with his fellow artist in New York about a joint concert, featuring himself, Dylan and Paul Simon, live on-stage in Port-au-Prince. He has no other plans for the town.

'I am a militant. A militant does not need to have plans,' is his formal position.

I tell him about the two potential investors who were looking to do business with him today.

'I don't like doing business. Investors are imperialists, every one of them. Best thing we can do is close the borders to people like that,' says the Mayor, absently strumming a few chords of 'Blowin' in the Wind'. The real wind, warm and full of litter, wafts in the distant sound of Bangladeshi blue helmets at evening prayer. Their entreaties continue long after the sun has gone down.

I decide to leave Uphold Democracy to its own devices and to head out for the UN's Opération Retour in Rwanda. A

UN soldier from Ireland is waiting for the same plane as me. He's going on R&R to the American state of Florida.

'I was driving through another of those miserable settlements,' he tells me. 'Right in the middle of the road, there's this ancient old lady, all wrinkled and bent. I can't get round her and have to step out of the car. She immediately grabs me and won't let me go. I finally understand that she's had a row at home. Her husband has called down a voodoo curse on her. She is doomed to shrink, a little more every day, until there is nothing left of her. She will be smaller than a grain of rice, she says. And could I help her, *s'il vous plaît*? She's shaking with misery.

'So, there I am, still with no blue helmet to hide under. I should have said, "Sorry old lady, but you have to go to the police, who don't really exist yet." That's what I should have said. But instead I say, "Madame, the UN knows what to do. We have just what you need. This anti-curse powder. Success guaranteed." And I give her a packet of lemonade powder from US Army rations. "Every day, one lick," I say, "swallow it down well and you won't shrink another inch." She thanked me a hundred times, kissed my hands, kissed my feet. As if I were the messiah. That old lady is still haunting me. Because just for a moment, I even believed it myself, because it would have been so wonderful. For a moment I really believed I was working miracles. But actually it was just another cheap trick. Just like the Americans: "The UN knows what to do . . . success guaranteed . . ." Those poor bastards really believe in miracles and I go along with it. Just to get rid of them.'

## 4. The UN in Rwanda: The End

*I*

### UN bureaucracy fails in Rwanda

Nobody can say that General Dallaire (the Canadian UN Force Commander in Rwanda) did not do his best. On 11 January 1994 he sent a telegram to the Head of Peacekeeping Operations in New York, reporting that extremists in Rwanda were fomenting civil war. He also predicted the genocide. All the Tutsis in Kigali were being registered with an eye to their extermination. New York replied the same day. Dallaire should take no action against the extremists. Such 'offensive operations', it was argued, fell outside the mandate that the Security Council had issued to blue helmets in Rwanda.                (*De Morgen*, 17 January 1996)

Three months after his telegram, Rwanda was overtaken by the events that the UN Commander had foreseen. In spite of the peace accords that had been signed and the 2,500-man UN force put in to supervise their observance, the civil war in Rwanda flared up again and more bloodily than ever before.

### Belgium pulls its troops out of Rwanda

Kigali, 14 April 1994 – 'Belgian blue helmets will not stay under any circumstances.' With these words the Belgian Foreign Minister Willy Claes yesterday put an axe to the roots of the UN mission in Rwanda. Several hundred Belgian blue helmets have formed the linchpin of the 2,500-strong UN force.

'The mission has absolutely no point any more. Blue helmets have not been able to prevent more than 20,000 people being killed in a few days. And the situation is getting ever more chaotic,' said an emotional Claes. (*Trouw*)

Apart from 450 African blue helmets, all UN troops were rapidly withdrawn from Rwanda. Five weeks and an estimated 980,000 dead later, the Security Council decided, at the urgent request of France, to restore and then increase the number of blue helmets in Rwanda.

### Boutros admits UN failing in Rwanda

New York, 26 May 1994 – Boutros-Ghali yesterday admitted that the UN has not succeeded in finding the extra soldiers needed to bring the UN mission in Rwanda up to 5,500 men. 'I have failed,' said Boutros-Ghali. 'It is a scandal. I am the first to say it and I am ready to repeat it.' [. . .] An estimated one million people have already died in the Rwandan civil war. (*NRC Handelsblad*, AP)

While Boutros-Ghali continued to search for blue helmets, France decided not to wait.

### French invasion begins today

Paris, 23 June 1994 – The French Ministry of Defence has announced that Opération Turquoise, the French intervention in Rwanda, is already underway. Troops from the Foreign Legion and the French marines, in armoured vehicles and with helicopter cover, will enter western Rwanda from Zaire. The invasion force will pull out again in two months, on 22 August. A UN peacekeeping force will then take over the mission.          (Reuters)

A month after the French invasion, no blue helmets for Rwanda had yet been found.

### Hutus flee to French 'safe haven'

Brussels/Goma, 19 July 1994 – The Tutsi rebel army, the RPA, has declared itself the winner of the civil war. The RPA has control of the whole country, except for the 'safe haven' that the French army has established in the south-west. Hundreds of thousands of Hutu refugees are now living in this so-called Zone Turquoise.          (AFP, AP)

Another month later, and 6,000 blue helmets had finally been scraped together. The ambitious goal of their mission, christened Opération Retour, was to persuade all the Hutus seeking refuge in Zone Turquoise to return to their villages.

### Rwanda sends army to safe haven

Kigali, 19 August 1994 – The new Rwandan Premier, M. Twagiramungu, has declared that the RPA soldiers will enter Zone Turquoise as soon as the French have left. The new government of Rwanda is not planning to let UN troops take over. 'The UN recognizes our sovereignty,' said the Premier. 'Zone Turquoise forms an integral part of Rwanda and it is up to the Rwandan army to ensure order and security there.' The Rwandan army is said to be ready to co-operate with blue helmets.                                    (*Guardian*)

## II

*Rwanda, March 1995*

Rivers full of bodies and vast herds of refugees: even though the genocide is already a year in the past, it is proving hard to shift the tourist image of Rwanda back to gorilla safaris. The new Rwandan government is therefore insisting that the war is now over and that the gorillas can go back in the brochures. The World Wildlife Fund (WWF) is supporting the promotion.

'Tourist dollars must jingle, otherwise it's impossible for us to keep the Rwandans convinced that our Save the Gorillas Project has any value,' sighs José Kalpers of the WWF's Gorilla Preservation Project. The matter is urgent: the creatures are on the point of extinction and their only territory lies right in the heart of the war zone. Although Rwanda is now blessed with a UN Peace Mission, the war is still dragging on and no PR man can conjure away that reality.

Thanks to the film *Gorillas in the Mist* (1988), the story of American biologist Dian Fossey who lived with the gorillas for thirteen years, the great apes were an important source of income for Rwanda. Gorilla lovers had been queuing up to visit them until April 1994, when the massacres began, after which Rwanda's gorillas were engulfed in the flood of war victims.

Now, a year after the genocide, six European journalists have been invited to observe the peace in Rwanda with their own eyes. During a special five-day promotional tour through gorilla country (the Ruwenzori mountains, which Rwanda shares with Zaire and Uganda) they will be free to describe and photograph the gorillas to their heart's content. The aim is to get a picture of furry apes on misty volcanic slopes to slide over the image that won the World Press Photo award: a portrait of a mutilated Rwandan war victim. A Belgian reporter and a French photographer have duly presented themselves in the capital, Kigali, but at the last minute the other *invités* have been redirected by their editors to cover yet another outbreak of hostilities between Hutus and Tutsis, this time in neighbouring Burundi. I am therefore allowed in to make up the numbers.

First item on the programme is an audience with the Director of Rwanda's Parc National des Volcans. 'You are much too late for a war story, madame,' he informs me, smiling broadly. '*La sécurité est totale.* Tourists have nothing to fear!' Director Alype Nkundiyareme expresses his enthusiasm loudly in order to be heard over the roar of UN trucks passing under his window. Tightly knotted around his neck is a tie sporting the panda logo of the WWF. On his desk, a little bronze gorilla, gracefully stretching like a pin-up: a paperweight for papers that aren't there. The gorilla booking office, like all the other public buildings in Rwanda, was plundered during the war. Since then nobody has booked for gorilla safaris unless, like M. Nkundiyareme, you count the aid workers and blue helmets who sometimes spend their free weekends up in the Parc.

'What kinds of animals, apart from gorillas of course, can be seen in the Parc des Volcans?' we ask, pens poised above notebooks. No answer. The question has taken the Director by surprise. His brown eyes flick uneasily round the room. They pass over a faded *Gorillas in the Mist* poster and finally settle on a school biology lesson chart that has been pinned over the bullet holes in the wall. 'Primates in Rwanda' it says, above educational pictures of various kinds of ape. The Director leans forward for a better view.

'We have . . . er . . . primates,' he gasps, much relieved.

The man is new to his job, as is virtually the whole framework of government in Rwanda. The Tutsis who wielded the sceptre up until April 1994 have been murdered, almost to a man. The Hutus, including the ex-President and his entire cabinet, have fled to camps in Zone Turquoise, and to neighbouring Zaire, Tanzania and Burundi.

Vacant posts are handed out to new arrivals: Tutsis who have returned from exile. Most have not been here since 1959, when the Hutu government of the day raised bloody persecution of Tutsis to the level of national policy. The majority of these 'diaspora Tutsis' can barely manage to find their way home from the office. Nor are there remotely enough of them. The Ministry of Tourism and the Environment, just like the Parc office, are still running on half the required staff, and these are not qualified for their functions.

The audience with the Director is apparently at an end: 'Just write that tourists can come again without worries, *en masse.*' He hopes we enjoy the gorillas and shepherds us, gently but firmly, out of the door. We might get it into our heads to ask about Rwandan plants, about which there is no school chart.

At the reservation desk a UN soldier from Austria is waiting impatiently for a receipt. He has just paid $126 for a ticket to enter the Parc. The receptionist can't find the receipt pad anywhere. She too is new. The UN soldier drums his fingers on the desk. 'Now and then we just need a bit of diversion, otherwise we go crazy from all the victims in this country. Last year's dead are still lying in the streets in our district. But at least they're not oozing any more. The stink of skeletons is much easier to take,' he says.

The Kahuzi Biega forest begins halfway up the slopes of the eight volcanoes. It is here that the gorillas are supposed to be roaming, though nobody knows how many of them are still left. International conservation organizations first began to take an interest in the declining population at the start of the 1980s, after which gorilla numbers increased from 500 to 600. Or so the WWF guesses. Now, with the WWF panda on the door of his Land Rover and three boxes of warden kit in the back, José Kalpers drives lazily up the mountain road which winds up from Kigali towards Ruhengiri, a hundred or so kilometres to the north. He's hoping to find the warden's HQ still manned. Apart from columns of white-painted trucks on their way to the camps, there is no other traffic on the road. Now and then we pass a Tutsi farmer, out grazing his cattle or goats. '*Biscuit! Biscuit!*' call the children playing by the road. We are entering Zone Turquoise, which Zambian blue helmets took over a couple of months ago from French commandos.

At a crossroads halfway to Ruhengiri, we find a food distribution point run by a charity organization. It is suddenly teeming with people, jostling each other with identical red buckets, gifts from another charity. A UN Opération Retour truck, carrying a group of refugees being repatriated from Zaire, comes hissing to a halt. A Hutu family jumps down on to the road. Some buckets are thrown out after them. They wave to the departing truck and join the queue for food.

We drive on. Again the road is exclusive to us and the aid workers. We pass CARE and UNICEF jeeps and a truck full of Ethiopian blue helmets. On the surrounding hilltops I can see Rwandan soldiers, their binoculars scanning the Zairean side of the mountain.

'There is some attention for Nature again in Rwanda,' Kalpers is claiming. 'During the war everyone had other things on their mind. I was evacuated to Nairobi myself. Nobody was sure of their lives any more, not even foreigners.'

When the Tutsi RPA defeated the former Hutu regime, the all-clear was sounded. Kalpers came back to Rwanda, only to find that the WWF centres along the rim of the Parc had been flattened and plundered. Of his eighty wardens, no trace.

'Twenty-five of them have since reappeared. But anyone not back by now won't be coming. They'll be dead.' He ponders: 'Or fled and afraid. But more likely dead.'

Jerking his thumb towards the three big boxes in the back, he explains, 'New uniforms for my men. If you want to motivate your staff, then you've first got to ensure that they can do their work properly. Wardens can't go out on patrol without respectable tents, rifles, radio transmitters and the right clothing. All stolen during the war. Today they'll at least get new boots and warm sweaters from me, because it's cold and wet out on these volcanoes. Yes, things are looking up again for Nature in Rwanda. The new government has made conservation a priority. They appreciate the ecological importance of the gorilla forest, thank God.'

His words are still hanging in the air as we pull up sharply in front of a Tutsi-government-army roadblock. And it soon begins to look as if the festive hand-over of new warden clothing is off. Beaming warden faces would have provided some nice promotional pictures for our team of journalists, but they're not going to be taken today. With boxes and all, we are conveyed to Ruhengiri's football stadium. Our Land Rover with its panda logo is closely escorted by soldiers on back-firing mopeds and by others in pickup trucks fitted with mortar-launchers. These vehicles are painted in psychedelic yellow blotches, as if the army were camouflaging itself for a custard-pie war. Kalpers has pulled out all the stops to explain that there are wardens up there on the volcano, and that they are freezing to death, but the soldiers are not impressed. Nor do they believe him. What Kalpers calls 'work clothes' look far more combat-appropriate than the 'uniforms' they're wearing themselves – a motley collection of second-hand civilian jackets above camouflage trousers, dented helmets above darned socks. The new Tutsi government has managed to recruit its forces more rapidly than it can dress them. Soldiers in flip-flops, silent with admiration, finger each pair of unworn, military-green, profile-soled jungle boots to appear from the boxes. Then come the water bottles, belts and green woollen sweaters with leather shoulder pads. They are all caressed, then counted, then confiscated.

One of the soldiers leans through the window of the Land Rover to chat to me in English. He began his military career in Rwanda four months ago, he tells me, but before that he was at secondary school in Uganda. He picks up my passport from the dashboard and studies the photo.

'Is that you, or him?' he points to Kalpers. 'We find it hard to tell *blancs* apart. To you, all *nègres* look the same, right? A Ugandan friend of mine travelled all over Europe on my passport. Waved through every border, no problem.'

I change the subject and ask him the point of the roadblock.

'Things happen,' he says.

'What kind of things? Are the Hutus in the camps planning an attack?'

Too late I realize that this was not a sensible question. I've not been in Rwanda long enough to have internalized the universal fear: the enemy has fled, but has not been defeated. In the camps of Zone Turquoise there are still more than 200,000 Hutus. With reinforcements from the Hutu legions based in Zaire, a sizeable invasion army could be assembled. Zaire is within walking distance of here.

The Tutsi soldier springs back in alarm: 'Do you have information that we don't have?' he demands.

Kalpers distracts our attention. 'Here! All the papers are in order and signed by your own government,' he blusters to an officer in a red beret.

'In Rwanda nobody wanders around in military green. Except for the army, of course,' replies the officer calmly.

Near by the Belgian journalist is trying to persuade his interrogator that our aim is not to supply the Hutu enemy, but to visit gorillas. He points to the volcano, Nyiragongo, whose glowing summit is about to disappear in the clouds. 'We want to write a story about the gorillas and make the world aware that the war is over and that it's safe again to be a tourist in Rwanda.'

The soldier looks at the volcano, then at the reporter, shakes his head in pity and walks off.

When we are finally allowed through to see the gorillas in the Parc des Volcans it is twenty-four hours later and Kalpers has quit as tour leader. Maybe he could have restrained us from photographing the female gorilla found dead in the jungle a few days before. The wardens have dragged her off the steep, muddy slopes of the volcano for an autopsy. She is now peeled out of the jute sack into which she's been sewn, and hoisted upright between two bamboo poles for the benefit of our cameras. Pathos drips from the image. There is no doubt that photo editors, trying to match something to articles on conservation in Rwanda, will find it far more compelling than pictures of the reforestation project that is our next stop on the programme. And a few hundred seedlings in plastic pots aren't going to enhance the reputation of any photographer.

★

In the summer of 1994 the west of Rwanda emptied as refugees streamed towards the town of Goma in Zaire. The Hutu population was being driven away by the advancing Tutsi army. The only major road to the border was quickly dubbed the 'cholera highway' as traffic became totally jammed by victims of the disease. In their haste and determination to reach the camps in Goma, people stumbled between cars and carts piled high with household goods and over the bodies of their fellow refugees. Thirty thousand people an hour came past the Zaire customs post at the border, for days on end. A board from that time still remains in the verge of the road. It reads: 'Attention! Refugees! 10 kph.'

Hutu radio had announced that the pursuing Tutsis were cooking and eating Hutu refugees. Panic-stricken Hutus, held up by the vast tailback of humanity, took short cuts through the gorilla forest covering the lower slopes of the volcanoes. That July, José Kalpers had told us, he'd several times flown up to Goma from his refuge in Nairobi. From the air he'd seen streams of Hutus pushing their way along the narrow jungle paths, reaching the final bamboo thickets and pouring out into the camps in the Goma valley.

'Tens of thousands of them!' Kalpers would never forget it. 'Luckily they kept to the lower paths to reach Goma as quickly as possible. So the gorillas were able to sit high up near the crater and wait for the flood to subside.'

Tourists looking for gorillas on the Zairean side of the reserve would now get hopelessly stranded in the permanent queue of vehicles bringing in aid. The valley at the foot of Nyiragongo is crammed full of tents and huts made from banana leaves. Blue plastic tarpaulins provided by UNHCR, the UN's refugee organization, are draped over them to keep out the daily downpours.

Goma had long been an important trading centre in the

Eastern Zaire region, but the town had never amounted to much. Even with 200,000 inhabitants, it was little more than a sleepy village. A thousand metres of motorway, a petrol station, a landing strip and a bank, and that was Goma.

The Rwandan Hutus have turned the town into a metropolis. If you count the original inhabitants and the aid workers, the population is now almost 1.5 million and growing every day, with Hutu refugees from Burundi also swelling the numbers. Transport planes, their holds full of aid, their scream deafeningly low over the centre of town every few minutes.

The *gardiens* of the Parc National Virunga are despondent. The refugees have descended like a swarm of locusts and are rapidly eating their way upwards out of the valley, straight through the reserve. And there is nothing the *gardiens* can do to stop them.

'They begin by sawing off the branches, then they chop down the trees and finally rip the stumps, roots and all, out of the ground. So after deforestation, we'll soon be getting erosion,' complains Bisidi a *gardien* at the Parc National Virunga. He stomps angrily ahead of us through the valley.

It feels like I'm inside one of those United Colors of Benetton posters. Lines of Hutus, like ants, are crossing the shoulders of the through road to Bukavu and entering the reserve, axes, saws and machetes at the ready. A second long line is on the way back from the jungle to the city of huts, plundered firewood balanced on their heads. All, to the tiniest refugee toddler, are so heavily loaded that one more twig would be too much. Thick stumps and tree trunks chopped into sections are lashed with vines to planks on wooden wheels. The sound of hammers and saws, wielded by hundreds of carpenters, reverberates from the surrounding mountains.

'*Les réfugiés* have even started a furniture-making business,' says Bisidi. He points in angry triumph at a procession of women and children who have hoisted wooden tables and benches on to their heads and are off to find customers in Goma Ville. There are huts right up to the rim of the protected forest 'The current rim,' mutters Bisidi.

'The jungle used to begin right here at the edge of the road. Now all you can see are bushes. For trees you've got to walk kilometres.' The suffocating smoke from the cooking fires of more than a million people hangs motionless in the valley, a silent witness to the disaster that is rapidly unfolding. The refugees are burning a kilo and a half of wood per person per day. The UN have brought in Michel Leusch, a Swiss ecologist, to measure the scale of the catastrophe. He has never seen anything like it.

'We spent a week outside the camps weighing all the firewood that was brought in from the reserve. And we found they were consuming a mind-blowing 1,050 tons of protected wood every day. And the local population's respect for conservation has also disappeared in the process. Now they're all rushing after the Hutus with their axes to cash in before the wood has completely gone.'

When aid organizations decide to hand out food aid, maize and beans arrive in the disaster area uncooked. After all, food aid is food aid. Fuel aid is something else . . . 'But there's no such thing. Much too expensive,' says Leusch. 'Even the budgets for food aid are going down. Rations in the Goma camps were recently halved to a thousand calories per person per day.' I seem to remember that this is exactly the number of calories to which I condemn myself when my jeans get too tight round the belly.

'Anyway, this halving of rations made no difference at all to the consumption of firewood. Whether you cook a kilo of beans or a pound, it always takes two hours until they are done,' sighs the ecologist. He admits that a month ago firewood consumption was even higher, up around 2 kilos per person per day. But the reduction has nothing to do with a growing affection for nature. 'The refugees have to walk further and further to find any firewood. That's the only reason they're starting to be more economical with it.'

UN experts are racking their brains to find alternatives for the protected firewood. Should we bring wood to the Hutus, or the Hutus to the wood? The first option founders on impassable roads, the second on lack of money and organization.

'The only real solution is for the Hutus to go home,' says Leusch. That seems a non-starter. Between the leaf-huts of the camps you can find wooden house frames, which look very much as if they're intended for permanent habitation. There is even a two-storey structure waiting for cladding.

Maize and bean distribution has ended up in the hands of the former Hutu army, which has taken over the camps. Firewood distribution has gone the same way. The 'wood mafia' determines who fetches the merchandise and what should be paid for it. And they let nobody stand in their way, claim the *gardiens*. As a result of negotiations between the Zaire government in Kinshasa and the UN in New York, the refugees have permission to gather dead wood in the jungle for two days a week, because cooking has to be done. On the other five days the theft of wood simply goes on, but the *gardiens* don't dare to say anything: the first victims have already been claimed. Bisidi tells us about a colleague who had sent illegal gatherers out of the jungle. Hutu soldiers promptly paid him a house call. 'They cut up his little girl's arm with a machete, as a way of telling Daddy not to take any further interest in their affairs.' A Dutch UN official in Goma, one of twelve military observers sent to Zaire by Holland as part of Opération Retour, knows of a *gardien* who had an axe planted in his chest by wood poachers. And their boss, Conservateur Wathaut, claims that mines have been laid in the battle for firewood. '*Donc, c'est la guerre!*' Wathaut works himself up into a fury. 'The Hutus opened the Rwandan prisons before they fled and all that scum is here with us now in the camps.' The flaps of his safari helmet, acquired from a souvenir shop in Nairobi, hang down past his ears. In a corner of his office lie wooden spears, relics of a time when the battle in the gorilla forest was still confined to Wathaut's alert men and the occasional local poacher. Another such reminder hangs on the wall: a primitive painting of a *gardien* disabling a poacher with a blow to the head from his rifle. Gorillas look on gratefully from between the trees.

These days no *gardien* is surprised when a poacher pulls out a grenade, says Wathaut: the Rwandan ex-government army has been only partly disarmed in the camps. The soldiers now employ their weapons to protect wood thieves and charcoal burners against the Zairean *gardiens*. There is no proof of this hit-and-run jungle war, but rumours abound.

At this point the Belgian reporter asks if he can choose a souvenir from an untidy pile of machetes on the floor of the office – 2,000 of them, confiscated in 1994.

Monsieur le Conservateur pulls a wry face. '*Si vous voulez.* But remember that last year they were used by these same Hutus to hack their compatriots to death.'

There is a lot at stake for the groups fighting each other in the jungle. Clad in what remains of his uniform after months in the Goma camps, a Hutu emerges from the trees with a huge branch perched on his head. He tells us that he covers 30 kilometres like this every day. The wood fetches nearly a dollar.

If the refugees don't go home soon, the reserve will be gone for ever. Five thousand hectares have already been lost. With the trees, the gorillas disappear, and with the gorillas, the tourists, and with the tourists, Bisidi's job. 'At this rate, it will all be over in a month or so,' he says miserably.

The UN's Opération Retour is ticking over on the lowest possible revs. The groups being repatriated in giant UN trucks would easily fit into private cars. The staff of the IOM (the International Organization for Migration), who are assisting the UN in their attempts to persuade Hutus to go home, are slumped in their folding chairs behind their wooden tables, bored and staring. They are waiting for people who believe in the one-way trip. But there is far more interest being shown in the matches being played on the football pitches surrounding the camp.

'Innocent Hutus are welcome home,' is the message being constantly repeated by the Rwandan Tutsi government. But even the diplomatically cautious UN has, cautiously, expressed its concern over the mistreatment and disappearance of repatriates. There may be no evidence for the systematic murder of Hutus by the Tutsi army, but the camps are buzzing with rumours. Moreover, the Rwandan government seems to be bent on discouraging potential returnees. People here hold their breath as they listen to Rwandan radio informing them that more than 1,000 Hutus a week are being arrested on charges of involvement in the mass murder of Tutsis. The maximum capacity of Rwanda's prisons is 4,000. The Tutsis have already managed to cram them with 23,000 Hutus. There is no chance of a legal hearing: judges, public prosecutors and defence lawyers are either dead, in the camps, or have a price on their heads. The only way out of a Rwanda prison is in a body bag. So the Hutus prefer to remain what they are: refugees.

'We can't force them. As the UN, we can hardly tie them

up and throw them in the backs of our trucks, can we?'
demands a UN official as he sits waiting for today's volunteers.

Our gorilla promotion team resumes its safari. On the way up
from Goma to the Parc entrance at Bukima, we drive past a
funeral procession. Two bodies are being carried out of the
refugee camp on bamboo-pole biers.

'They dump them in our forest. Bad for the gorillas, they
could easily get infected, but *les réfugiés* don't care about that,'
moans Bisidi, airing another grievance.

No overnight tourist accommodation remains on the Rwandan side of the border since the war. The WWF guest bunga-
lows had their roofs stolen. The walls were then covered with
graffiti by the Hutu ex-government army, passing through
en route for Zaire, and finally shot to pieces. You can still
read 'Tutsis are cockroaches' scrawled in charcoal from their
fires.

On the Zaire side, however, a luxurious log cabin has been
placed at our disposal. In the back garden we find some of the
Hutu wardens whom José Kalpers so badly needs back in the
Parc des Volcans. They fled over the volcano last year and
have since been camping out close to their Zairean colleagues.
Eleven families, seventy people in all, living in huts made of
leaves, just like the hundreds of thousands the optimistic tourist
thought he had left behind in Goma.

One man, as far as he knows, is still employed by the
prestigious Dian Fossey Research Centre on the other side of
the border. The only evidence he can come up with in support
of his claim is an encyclopedia of birds. He has lost all his other
possessions – half of them during his flight to Zaire, the rest
in his flight from fellow Hutus who had got wind of his plan
to return home.

He produces a '*Liste des matériels que j'ai perdu*' in copybook script. This includes two tubes of Colgate toothpaste with toothbrush, '*Huit Mille Francs Rwandais avec Dix Dollars*' (a tip left by a pre-war safari-goer) and '*Deux bandes de cassette avec les chansons des oiseaux*'. He was busy learning these birdsongs by heart, to improve the service he could offer to tourists, when the Tutsis chased him over the volcano.

Next morning I choose to stay back at the WWF cabin, while the others go off in search of a family of Zairean gorillas. When they are late to return, the cabin staff begin to speculate about an unwelcome encounter with poachers. Zairean. Or maybe Rwandan, after wood, or it could be bushmeat. Or with Hutus on the way to destroy Tutsi targets in Rwanda. Unless it was Tutsi spies sneaking down into Hutu camps in Zaire. Or possibly with ordinary cattle thieves, who could come from anywhere. There seems to be no end to such sinister comings and goings.

When, hours later, the party reappears through the bamboo thickets exhausted and muddy, it turns out that the hold-up was due to a couple of Pygmies, caught red-handed on an illegal firewood expedition. After being relieved of their machetes, which will be added to the gruesome pile in Wathaut's office, and receiving a smart kick up the arse, the Pygmies were ordered to beat a retreat.

Almost at the end of our promotional tour, we encounter some genuine gorilla lovers. There are three of them, who have backpacked right up from South Africa and are now stuck at the rusty barrier manned by Zairean customs. Instead of military decorations, their jackets sport CNN badges, gifts from the camera teams who came through on their way to cover last year's cholera outbreaks in the camps. The arrival of the South Africans is a golden chance for the Zaireans.

They have already made a profit of $50 and a penknife, but are still not ready to stamp a visa for Goma.

The South Africans must think they are going to get it sorted out today, because they are keen for me to tell them about accommodation in Goma. What they would really like, they say, is to save on their expedition expenses by putting up their tent somewhere.

'Goma is one big camp site,' I assure them. And greatly cheered, they resume their negotiations with the customs officers.

Before we are allowed back to our desks to begin the task of recruiting gorilla-loving tourists, the Rwandan government wants us to accompany them on just one more trip; this time to witness them clearing mines in the Parc des Volcans. It would never have occurred to me personally, but the paltry numbers of tourists arriving in an area now declared safe might be due to fear of the explosives that are strewn all over the country. At least, that is what the government hopes.

The thick morning mist has dissolved and rain pours down on the dense jungle from the dark clouds hanging over the summits of the volcanoes. The climate, with its 2,000 mm annual rainfall, does not contribute much to Rwanda's holiday spirit. The jungle trail is transformed into a muddy cataract. We slop along behind government military engineers. The explosives expert, a lad of no more than fifteen, rapidly locates two grenades and a mine. He spots them with the naked eye in a deep pool of mud. His mates look on as if they are watching a magician producing rabbits out of a hat, but I can't get rid of the feeling that these explosives have been put there for us to report.

Under the gaze of our cameras the young expert covers the three rusting items with sticks of dynamite. Then we slither smartly away down the hillside. The bangs must have had the gorillas trembling for days.

At the foot of the mountain I run into Shaharya Khan, the UN Special Representative. He is in his walking boots, with a raincoat under his arm and a flak jacket on the back seat of his car. You can never be sure in Rwanda.

'Nice weather!' he says, very friendly. He is on his way up to the Parc entrance in a convoy of seven jeeps (carrying Tunisian blue helmets) and three pickup trucks (crammed with nonchalantly smoking Tutsi-government soldiers). Khan has the day off today. So Director Nkundiyareme has at least one more tourist to swell his Parc statistics.

It is long after sundown and I am driving back into Kigali. Just one more military checkpoint to negotiate.

'Where are you coming from?' demands a teenage soldier.

'From the gorillas, monsieur,' I reply.

'Which gorillas?' he asks suspiciously, and shines his flashlight on to the back seat as if he expects to find one sitting there.

'The gorillas on the volcano,' I say.

'What gorillas?'

Only later did the question strike me. Yes, indeed. What gorillas?

## III

*Rwanda, April 1995*

A week later and 80 kilometres to the east, I find myself back in the middle of UN's Opération Retour, this time with my left foot on the body of a Hutu refugee just shot by a Tutsi soldier. I am scared and wishing I could hide behind the broad back of Captain Max, US Special Forces in Haiti. Max would have wiped the disgusting grins from these murderers' faces and then shot them dead, no doubt about it. But now it's only Captain Francis, of the United Nations. He stands straddling the bodies of other refugees who lie dying, riddled with bullets. Opposite us, the gunmen, Rwandan government soldiers.

UN Commander Francis Sikaonga is a giant of a man by any standards. And now he has puffed himself out and stretched every sinew to achieve even greater proportions. He towers a good 2 metres above the bodies at his feet, with his huge hands planted indignantly to his sides and his chest, emblazoned with the UN emblem, thrust out in challenge. The Captain is doing his best to impress, but has already been exposed as an impotent missionary. Does he have any cards left to play?

'You're only an observer in Rwanda,' one of the government soldiers has snapped at Francis, as he tried to interfere in the shooting. 'A guest. You're not the boss here. We are the bosses.'

'You must allow me to help these people,' the Captain is saying. He manages to make it sound like an order. I keep pressed to his back and wait for the shot.

The government soldiers snigger. A few shake their heads in pity. One doesn't listen at all: he is absently poking his gun into the belly of one of his victims.

'If you don't let me help these people, they are going to die!'

It sounds like a threat. The government soldiers pretend to be shocked, and then burst out laughing.

'So . . . what about it?' says one of them.

'You can't . . . just let people die . . .'

'Oh yes we can,' says a soldier, already bored. 'You know that very well.'

## IV

Shoulder to shoulder, on a mountain plateau the size of three football pitches, stand 150,000 refugees. By the time I find them, they have been there for sixty hours. Apparently, somewhere in this sea of humanity, there are two small camps occupied by ZamBat, UN peacekeepers from Zambia, but I can see no sign of them.

There is no room to sit down on the plateau. The refugees stand pressed together, on top of each other's possessions and straddling the bodies of old people and children who are too tired to stay on their feet. Government soldiers in long raincoats, some wearing black berets, rifles slung over their shoulders, stand in a cordon around the vast huddled mass, one every 10 metres. Kibeho, the largest refugee camp on Rwandan soil, was closed by these soldiers the day before yesterday on orders from the government. Opération Retour was taking too long. Government soldiers chased the inhabitants out of their huts in the surrounding valleys and herded them on to the plateau, where they are holding them under guard.

After successfully clearing the camp, the Tutsi soldiers have apparently run out of orders. They've been standing here just like the refugees for two and a half days, waiting for someone to tell them what to do next with these Hutus. The soldiers draw with their sticks in the dust, take drags on each other's cigarettes, and yobbishly kick discarded Hutu possessions into the deep valley below. I look down. It is as if a hurricane has swept through the place. Tens of thousands of huts have been knocked over and trampled. Some are burned out. Cooking pots, rice baskets and muddy blankets are strewn between the vague piles that used to be huts. Here and there a soldier pokes through the abandoned gear to see if there's anything he fancies.

Somewhere deep in the crowd, people start pushing. An old woman is shoved off the packed plateau and rolls on to the road which runs just under the rim, towards me. Freely wielding their sticks, the soldiers drive her back into the mass.

A group of blue helmets emerges from the fringe of the crowd: my escort to one of the ZamBat camps. So the UN is still here, then.

'We have to go straight through. Take a deep breath while you still can,' advises one of the blue helmets. I push after them into the crowd. The refugees are numb with misery. They do not hear the blue helmets shouting 'Make way!' and they don't feel it when they are roughly pushed aside. Laboriously, step by step, we worm our way deeper into the multitude. Whichever way I look, I see only heads, with dull eyes and lips white with thirst. Under my feet the floor is covered with indeterminate baggage, amongst which I occasionally encounter a person. You can't see the ground any more. At first I am cautious, trying to find a place to put my feet with every step, but then I get scared of being left behind. I must be less scrupulous and not care too much about what or who I am stepping on. '*Pardon, pardon,*' I hear myself mumbling a thousand times. As I feel my feet sink into anything soft, I just hope it's not somebody. Or excrement. For sixty hours the refugees have been forced to relieve themselves where they stand or have fallen. The stench literally takes my breath away.

Suddenly, a pair of muddy legs pokes up from under a blue tarpaulin. I stumble, lose my balance and fall against the filthy people. By the time I regain my feet, the legs have merged back into the blankets and wet mattresses which the fleeing Hutus have managed to drag up to the plateau. The path forged by the blue helmets has disappeared. I am stranded, with no idea which way to go. As panic seizes me, a hand grabs my wrist. A blue helmet pulls me through the wall of people. Hyperventilating, I hang on to his belt with both hands for the rest of the strenuous wade through the human sea.

We finally reach a red and white pole that serves as a barrier. Behind it stands Kibeho's former primary school, in which UN Commander Francis Sikaonga and his eighty soldiers are based.

Just as the Tutsi soldiers are keeping their Hutu prisoners surrounded to stop them escaping the plateau, the Zambian blue helmets are surrounding the school to stop the Hutus from flattening it. Behind rolls of barbed wire, the Zambians form a cordon around their car park, the former school playground, which is just big enough for the three white jeeps that are parked there. The metal gates of the school, heavily dented, are locked and guarded by Zambians.

The refugees are trying to get as close to the UN soldiers as they can. They bulge, barbed wire and all, on to the car park. Some have won themselves a place to sit down. Their legs are stretched out as far as possible under the wire, as if to ensure that at least their lower halves are on safe ground. The refugees say nothing and do nothing but stare at the Zambians.

I approach a blue-helmeted soldier in shirt sleeves. He is using a wrench on a water pump, which lies in a twisted heap on the ground. 'Flattened when these people stormed our camp two days ago,' he explains. His voice is angry, but his eyes are pained as he looks towards children who wait with parched open mouths under the waste pipe, in the vain hope of catching a drip.

Two nights ago, he says, there were sudden salvos of rifle fire. 'We immediately got into position behind the sandbags, because we had no idea who was shooting at whom. Maybe we were the target ourselves. Then we felt the earth trembling and thought it was tanks. Until we realized that it was tens of thousands of people, running. We couldn't really believe it, until we saw this crowd scrambling up towards us. They came from all sides, screaming, straight at us, with I reckon a thousand government soldiers shooting behind them. Our commander stayed perfectly calm. It is thanks to him that we didn't start shooting too, out of sheer terror, not even when the refugees finally stormed right through the barbed wire and into the camp. I really thought we'd all had it.'

His voice has grown hoarse: 'We just had time to climb on the sandbags and then on to the roof of the school. Everywhere we saw people stumbling, falling on top of each other and being trampled to death. There's the evidence . . .' He nods towards lumpy forms under blue tarpaulins, laid out neatly beside the barrier. A Zambian soldier is just walking up to them, holding a woman by the arm. He lifts the sheets one by one so that she can see what's underneath: eleven children, trampled in the nocturnal stampede. The woman shakes her head. She has lost her child, but it's not here. The Zambian leads her back to the barbed wire. She twists herself underneath, presses her back into the wall of people and stands there immobile, her gaze fixed on the Zambians.

The stampede was finally broken by the walls of the school. When the Zambians had dared to come down from their refuge, it had taken them hours to direct the refugees back to the other side of the flattened barbed wire. ZamBat was just dragging the last bodies away from the school gates when government soldiers approached Captain Francis.

'We are taking over this position. The refugees are going home,' they announced. How the refugees were going to get there the soldiers did not say, and that remains a mystery.

They are not allowed to walk home because the Rwandan government is afraid that they will stop a few kilometres down the road and set up a new camp. Loading them into trucks and taking them back to their villages is not an option, because the government has no trucks. The UN, which does have a few in Rwanda, is not allowed to assist in the deportation of prisoners. The UN has to be sure that their passengers are going home voluntarily, and there is no question of that with these people.

The two roads which wind through the mountains to Kibeho have been closed by the government army. Food and water convoys, sent by the aid organizations who were working with the refugees in Kibeho, are being turned back. As of the day before yesterday, all aid has been officially forbidden.

'We've been standing here for sixty-two hours now,' says the blue helmet, 'waiting for someone to start doing something.' He nods to the people behind the barbed wire. 'They're hoping it will be us. We're hoping it will be God. But it is the Rwandan government that will have to come up with a solution. It's their country. We're not allowed to interfere.'

Suddenly angry, he hurls his wrench to the ground and gropes wildly around in the toolbox. 'These people have had nothing to eat or drink for two days. They are going out of their minds with thirst. They think that I'll give them water when I have repaired this pump, but we have barely enough for ourselves.' Supplies for the eighty Zambians are being held back at the roadblocks, just like supplies for the refugees.

An American working for UNICEF, allowed through because he had no aid with him, is deep in conversation with Captain Francis. He has almost persuaded the local Tutsi-government commander that the Hutus will have to be given water if he's to get them to leave – however that is supposed to happen. His argument is that people can go without food for a while, OK, but if they're half dead with thirst you'll never get them to move.

'There's a tanker with 18,000 litres of drinking water up at the roadblock, 10 kilometres away. If the Tutsis say Yes, that water can be here within half an hour.'

'That's fine,' says Captain Francis, 'except that you won't be able to distribute it. The Rwandan soldiers have smashed all the pumps they could find in Kibeho. We'll try to repair a few for you. But there's not much more we can do.' Francis calls five of his soldiers out of the cordon and sends them off into the crowd with the UNICEF man and some tools. Then he too disappears. I just catch his voice saying: 'I must try to negotiate. There must be someone in charge here who can be brought to his senses.'

Why bother to share out water when there are only 18,000 litres for 150,000 dehydrated refugees? That's a decilitre, half a cup, per parched throat. To keep them all on their feet until tomorrow morning, you'd need at least 450,000 litres, 3 litres per refugee. And then, of course, another 450,000 litres tomorrow.

And how do you share out 18,000 litres between 150,000 people? By hand. Cup by cup. There is no alternative. Because the blue helmets haven't managed to repair even one of Kibeho's taps. These have been far too comprehensively smashed to yield to a UN-issue pipe wrench.

And how fast must you work to pour a cup of water for 150,000 people? Cups which won't be lying about in the Zambian camp. Francis's sigh comes from the depths of his being.

'OK, then, bring up your tanker,' he says to the American. 'We'll see what we can do.'

The tanker pulls into the car park with people hanging from the sides, licking droplets from the welding seams. The giant reservoir has a little brass tap halfway along. The blue helmets twist it open and start filling cups, tins and pans that are thrown to them by the crowd behind the wire. Then they carry the filled cups, tins and pans back to their owners, who wait sobbing with anticipation. As the ground below the tap gets muddy, a blue helmet slips and falls. The water from the cups he has just filled sloshes all over him. Scrambling to his feet, he goes back to the end of the queue of blue helmets awaiting their turn at the tap.

I have no idea how this humanitarian operation is supposed to succeed, but what I see these blue helmets clumsily trying, I can try too.

'We are the world . . .,' I hear myself humming, as I pick up my first empty tin from the ground and hold it under the thin stream from the tap. '. . . we are the children.' I carry the full tin to the barbed wire and hold it up until an owner claims it with a loud '*Merci!*'

'. . . so let's start giving,' a Zambian joins in. The illusion that we are saving the refugees makes us quite euphoric. We discuss how it can be done faster and better. We find an empty oil drum in the ZamBat kitchen. The cook, who hasn't been outside the school gates today, asks us to bring it back before six because he needs it to prepare ZamBat's dinner.

We attach a hose to the tanker and fill up the drum. Some of us dip the vessels thrown by the refugees into the water. Others go trotting back and forth to the wire with what we have filled. Meanwhile the remaining ZamBat soldiers stand guard over the crowd. The sight of the water, and then having to wait their turn for a sip, is too much for most of the refugees. They press ever closer to us, panting. The barbed wire bulges dangerously and the people who get stuck in it wail and scream. The Zambians on our side of the wire, who are growing increasingly panicky themselves, appeal for calm. 'Everybody will get a turn,' they lie desperately. At the back we see government soldiers chasing away people who've got hold of water by beating them over the heads with their sticks. When the tanker is completely empty, a few hundred of the 150,000 people on the plateau have gulped something down. Those whose turn never came stand pleading and weeping behind the barbed wire. Everybody is numb with exhaustion.

I am soaked and shivering.

The first time I witness the most extreme consequence of the UN's principle of non-intervention, I am furious. With the blue helmets. We watch as a group of refugees, half a dozen or so, break away from the crowd and make a run for it into the valley. They are trying to escape the siege! The crack of the government soldiers' rifles follows immediately. We see the refugees fall. Dead. Their bodies roll, tumbling over the rocks, down to the floor of the valley and come to rest against the trampled huts.

'They are murdering them!' I scream at Captain Francis. 'Stop them! Do something!'

Francis turns to me, growling. 'Like what? Shoot those soldiers, I suppose?'

'Why not? Good idea,' I snap back.

Francis regains his composure. 'Of course we've considered that, right from the start. But it's not possible. They're better armed than us . . .'

'So do something else then, but do something!'

'There are a thousand of them, and eighty of us.'

'Call for reinforcements then.'

'We have done, but even if all the 6,000 blue helmets in

Rwanda arrived in Kibeho today, and even if they were draped with the kinds of weapons we can only dream about, we still couldn't fight. There are 150,000 civilians standing between us and the government forces. To hit a Rwandan soldier we'd have to fire right through them.'

I look around me: from here I can only see three of the 1,000 government soldiers who must be roaming the plateau somewhere. This trio is peering over the lip of the valley to see whether the bodies below are still moving. Apart from them, I see only the solid wall of people. Some do their best to hold my glance, to beseech me with their eyes. I avoid their gaze and search for gaps through which a relief force could shoot. But there aren't any.

'And imagine the panic if we opened fire,' Francis goes on. 'There would be a stampede. More people dead. The government soldiers would naturally respond. Even more dead.'

'OK, OK, OK, I get it. Sorry,' I say.

But Francis goes on unperturbed. 'And to keep it simple, I'm not even mentioning the fact that the mandate of the peacekeeping force in Rwanda does not sanction force. We have orders to co-operate with the Rwandan authorities, not to shoot at them.'

For a moment I think I've caught the Captain out.

'But surely you can if those authorities are killing innocent civilians right under your nose.'

'Not even then. No.'

I turn down what later proves to be the last chance of a lift out of Kibeho, with a couple of UN observers going back to UN HQ in Kigali to raise even more alarm. I am too fascinated. I watch the blue helmets watching the murders going on all around them, eyes wide with disbelief and mouths gaping, like they are screaming but I can't hear them. I remain watching until the sun has completely disappeared and it's pitch dark on the plateau. Captain Francis appears behind me.

'We eat in half an hour. Go and wash yourself first.' He invites me through the gates into the little school. Wash myself, while all those people are dying of thirst? And then eating, while the Hutus haven't had anything for almost three days? I feel my moral indignation boiling up again. Francis feels it too and has the counter-arguments ready before I can launch into him.

'This,' he says, indicating the school courtyard with a wave of his arm, 'is normality.' I catch sight of a soldier sweeping out the sleeping quarters, of another lathering the chin of a colleague. In the kitchen I see the cook chopping onions and whistling.

'Out there,' says Francis, jerking his thumb over his shoulder, 'is insanity. And probably cholera too. It is my job to keep the insanity and the disease on the other side of the gates. Whether or not people are dying out there, we have to stay on our feet. There is no point in us dying with them. So eating, drinking, washing and sleeping. That is what we have to do.'

ZamBat's quarters consist of just three small brick buildings with corrugated iron roofs. These form three sides of a court-yard, closed off at the end by the metal gates. The soldiers sleep in bunks in what used to be classrooms. Behind one of these dormitories, in a former broom cupboard, a little tub of hot water has been set ready for me, along with a hunk of soap. Francis slides his own yellow flip-flops under the wooden swing door.

'Make sure you scrub your hands well. They didn't give us any rubber gloves and everything and everybody outside could be infected!' he calls and disappears.

★

It says 'Officers' Mess' on the door of the staff room. In I go, wearing a clean T-shirt borrowed from the Captain. On the table, a clean plastic tablecloth (floral design) and steaming dishes.

'Ah, there she is,' says Francis contentedly from the head of the table. He is dressed in a neatly pressed uniform. His second-in-command, Innocent (even he has to laugh at his own name today), waits behind a plastic plate. Also at the table are two UN human rights observers, a Greek and a Dutch woman. They, like me, have asked Francis for somewhere to sleep tonight. They're working overtime.

The Captain does the honours. He piles our plates with rice and chicken and fills our tumblers with red South African wine from a four-litre pack. During the meal we refer euphemistically to 'the problem outside'. We call the multitude 'IDPs' – Internally Displaced Persons – UN jargon for 'refugees in their own country'. Through the brick wall of the mess we can hear IDPs being executed. First comes the shot, then the screams of the terrified bystanders. Before we have finished the wine, at least three people outside have been killed.

It is midnight. Francis and Innocent are lying under a table covered with radio equipment. With their arms crossed behind their heads, they are staring at speakers which produce only static. For the last few hours all contact with the outside world has been lost. Francis has lent me his camp bed, but I can't sleep either. Judging by what I can hear through the wall, no one in Kibeho can sleep. There are the normal sounds of the human sea: an unceasing whimpering, coughing and weeping. And the occasional flurry, as Hutus trying to escape under cover of darkness are captured and shot.

At three o'clock in the morning it begins to rain heavily.

For the rest of the night I hear nothing but the deafening clatter on the corrugated iron above my head.

When the sun rises and I walk out through the school gates, the refugees are still standing exactly as they were yesterday, shoulder to shoulder, only now they are drenched. The siege of Kibeho has been going on for seventy-six hours.

'Is there any help coming today? Have you heard anything?' asks a Zambian soldier.

'Must be. They'll have to start doing something soon.'

'Who?' asks the Zambian. Good question. Who?

I start remembering films about Nazi concentration camps: these apathetic, staring prisoners behind the barbed wire are just the same. A child has wormed his way towards us through the human wall and now stands in front of the barbed wire crying to break your heart. About five years old, I reckon.

'What is it, child?' asks the Zambian who is standing guard immediately opposite.

'*Papa et Maman tombés,*' says the child. It pushes a forearm up with the other hand and then lets it fall. Lifeless. Then it rolls up a ripped trouser leg and regards us full of expectation. We look at a little pink, flayed leg. It looks like a half-peeled banana, with the peel hanging down round the ankles.

'If somebody doesn't do something, that child is going to die,' says a Zambian. He reaches resolutely over the wire and lifts the infant into the car park.

'And what now?' I ask.

'Don't know. Stick the strips of skin back on and hope that they heal?'

Other children have seen the Zambian rescue and are now standing in front of us with their little arms stretched out, begging to be picked up. Most of them have wounds to which they try to draw our attention. Some are even worse than the banana leg. One child points to a large hole in its skull. Another has a piece of bone protruding from its shin. There are about ten of them. We lift them all into our camp. Yet more children work their way to the front. The ten in the car park become twenty. They press themselves against the blue helmets. We look at their lips, cracked and white from dehydration, but smiling happily. They think they have escaped death, now that they're with us.

'What should we do with them now?' I ask a Zambian soldier.

'Display them on top of the sandbags? Maybe their parents will come and collect them.' I very much doubt it: parents are now pushing their children under the wire with their own hands. Forty children have become a hundred. They sit on and around the bags of sand, dehydrated toddlers on the knees of wounded six-year-olds and all too filthy to touch. For days their excrement has run down their legs to the ground. Judging by the dried remnants, they all have diarrhoea. There is not a drop of water left in Kibeho, certainly not enough to clean up a sick child.

'We'll have a thousand of them soon,' says a Zambian.

'They need food.'

'Water, much more urgently.' We have neither to offer them.

'We should only allow in those who are really badly wounded or really seriously ill,' I suggest. A demented idea, which to my horror is immediately taken up by the Zambians. Whoever thinks up a plan, I notice, becomes responsible for carrying it out. So from now on, with every child that wants to get into the car park, the Zambians ask me hopefully whether it's in a bad enough state to qualify. My judgement is not only demanded, but acted upon. I am shocked to find myself deciding who stays and who is returned irrevocably over the barbed wire. Meanwhile, parents who have pushed children over to us make sure they disappear into the crowd before we can dump them back in their arms.

Apathetic, some bleeding, others shivering with fever. The children sit in rows along the wall of the school. Captain Francis frowns deeply.

'What a lot of them!' he says. We reckon 120.

'I don't understand it,' I say, feeling guilty. 'I've rejected so many.'

'Some government soldiers have just accused me of starting a refugee camp for children,' says Francis. 'I told them not to exaggerate, that we were only babysitting a few kids until we had found their parents. Now I see what they meant. I will have to explain it to them before they come to clear out this children's camp too.'

But before I see Francis again, the problem has solved itself. Shooting breaks out close by. Immediately, the children have disappeared, veteran survivors already. Later, one by one, they try to come back, but this time I impose the new, stricter admission criteria: they must be seriously wounded or critically ill.

This little fat boy, for example, I cannot allow to stay. He has slipped under the wire and is now hanging on to my trouser leg, pleading: 'I am all alone here! No maman, no papa, nobody!'

With his chubby legs and his muddy Bermuda shorts, his Nikes and his back-to-front baseball cap on his healthy round head, he looks like a tourist in a nightmare. But he's at least ten years old, and in my nightmare that's old enough to find your way out alive.

'I can't see any blood and you're sturdy enough,' I say, pinching the plump flesh under his T-shirt. I pry his hands loose from my leg and tell him he has to go.

★

The latrines in the valleys have been smashed. For days now people have been defecating on each other and on each other's baggage. When rows ensue, machetes are immediately produced from the junk on the ground. And used. The first children with machete wounds are now presenting themselves to ZamBat. Here and there the refugees hurl themselves on their captors with sticks and stones. The government soldiers react like maniacs: they pump whole magazines into one dead Hutu. Francis pleads for their lives, at least where the executions are taking place within the immediate neighbourhood.

Today Tutsi soldiers approached the Zambians begging for food and water. So they must be short of supplies too. 'Hungry soldiers are dangerous,' says Francis, 'but I gave orders to send them away empty-handed. I just couldn't find it in my heart to help them.'

Besides, a few filled bellies won't avert the disaster now. A decent solution would take too long. It's taken too long already. The soldiers have been standing all day in the burning sun and all night in the soaking rain, just like the IDPs. With every shower the Hutus' excrement swills off the plateau and over their boots. They're scared of cholera and beginning to realize that, if this goes on much longer, they may not get out alive themselves.

'There's only 1,000 of them against 150,000 of their mortal enemies, who are getting increasingly desperate,' says Francis. 'Refugees who think they have nothing left to lose will attack their guards, whether or not they are armed. If enough of them join in, the soldiers are finished. If they don't get their orders soon, they'll have to solve the problem on their own initiative. But they've got no more idea how to do it than we have.'

★

At dinner, rice, Captain Francis shakes the last drops out of the carton of South African *droë rooi*. Right next to us, on the other side of the wall, a shot explodes. Innocent jumps and knocks over his glass.

'What a pity,' says Francis in sympathy. Innocent stares at the little red pool, spreading over the tablecloth.

'To the problem outside. May God save them,' he says.

Midnight again. Shrinking from bullets and machetes, the crowd has shifted a few metres back and forth over the plateau. On our side this has won them a bit more room and the Tutsi soldiers have not managed to pack them in tight before darkness falls. These few extra decimetres per person have enabled the refugees to lie down for the first time since the siege began. With their knees drawn up, but all the same. And not all on top of each other. Some even next to their neighbours. They have crept under blue UN tarpaulins, which rise and fall to the rhythm of their breathing.

I tiptoe out to the Zambian soldiers who are standing guard by the barbed wire under soft yellow spotlights. I am trying to be as silent as possible, as if entering a crowded dormitory.

The Zambians ask me to roll them some cigarettes. Their smoking rations are also held up at the roadblocks. We whisper so as not to wake the people. For the first time we are seeing them lying down, sleeping, not dead, and this gives rise to an intense feeling of gratitude: finally, for a moment at least, we don't have to watch them suffering.

'It's so great that they're lying down, isn't it?' I whisper emotionally as I hand round the smokes. The Zambians nod and gaze round with pleasure.

'They must have been so tired . . .' says one of them.

'They were exhausted,' says his colleague.

'Well at least they'll have had a bit of rest by tomorrow, when it all starts again,' I say.

'It won't start again. I feel it in my heart. Tomorrow we'll suddenly see a convoy of trucks coming over the mountains to pick them up and take them home.'

We stand there in silence, smoking and thinking about trucks. Watching when someone, under their tarpaulin, turns in their sleep and sleeps on. We hear a snore, and somewhere else a tune, softly hummed: a Rwandan lullaby, thinks one of the Zambians. Tarpaulins rustle. A cough. Which degenerates into a hacking fit. A baby is woken and cries. The Zambians and I look at each other, alarmed, and hold our breath. God, don't let them all wake and stand up and go on with their misery. Let them lie there. Because we don't want to see it any more.

The baby stops crying. Just one final sob. Even in my relief, I don't dare let my breath out too fast.

At two o'clock in the morning the nightly downpour begins and the multitude stand. The shooting begins again too. But by then I am flat on my camp bed with my eyes clamped shut.

'Go and get the children. All IDPs must go home today. The soldiers have taken a decision. They are going to herd the crowd off the plateau and everyone has to go past our barbed wire. Maybe their families will recognize them,' says Francis.

It is 6 a.m. Last night fifty or so foundlings were granted refuge in the Zambian dormitory. When they sense that we now want to send them outside again, they resist like wild cats. A few try to hide under the bunks, others grab hold of the bed legs so tight that we have trouble tearing their little hands loose. But we are implacable. Those who refuse to walk, we carry out of the gates.

The siege of Kibeho has now lasted 100 hours. We have

entered the fifth day. The people are barely distinguishable from the goods they are clutching. Unrecognizable piles, uniformly muddy. The multitude shuffles past the Zambian camp in long rows. They are making for the 'exit', a narrow path leading up to a neighbouring plateau, where trucks could pull up and take on refugees. There are two or three on the way from the UN, into which you could cram maybe two or three hundred people. But it's by no means certain that these trucks will be able to make it all the way to Kibeho. The nightly rain has made the road virtually impassable and they're making slow progress. But the Tutsi soldiers are counting on a miracle. They are trying to drive all their prisoners straight to the next plateau, as if there were thousands of trucks on the way. The refugees take every step with extreme reluctance; there's a real chance that death is awaiting them at the end of their slow journey.

We climb up on the sandbags and see that the whole plateau has begun to move. An exodus is underway, and everyone will have to file past our little school. But as people stop to beseech our help one final time, blockages form in front of the barbed wire. As the multitude presses forward, people fall on top of each other in rapidly growing piles. Yet others throw down their mattresses and cooking pots and fight their way back towards buried loved ones, whom they struggle to pull to their feet. A child becomes impaled on the barbed wire underneath three adults.

'Keep moving,' scream the blue helmets from the sandbags, imploringly. 'Stay calm. Don't panic. It will all be OK if you just keep moving!'

'The Tutsis are going to kill us,' wails a woman and makes like she's cutting her own throat.

'Move, keep moving, for Christ's sake!' a blue helmet yells at her, while staring over the heads of the multitude towards

the other side of the plateau. I follow his gaze: far away we
see government soldiers trying to get people moving in our
direction, first with sticks and then by firing into the air. It
creates a wave motion, of people trying to escape from the
bullets. The wave begins to roll over the plateau towards us.
The people in front of us can't see what's happening back
there. They are still lying entangled in screaming heaps. The
wave comes upon us with terrible speed.

'Keep moving! Go! Go! Go!' screams the blue helmet,
trying to warn them, but the barrier has snapped with a bang
and the front of the human wave is rolling into the car park.
The barbed wire disappears under people and people disappear
under people. I leap from the sandbags and run for the gate.
Too late. The car park is already flooded. I am stranded.
People are grabbing at me and I start to fall. I'll go down under
their feet and be crushed. Zambian soldiers, heading back to
the gate, pull me loose and drag me with them. By the time
we have pushed the gates closed and hurled our weight against
them, some forty Hutus have managed to force their way in.
The people outside scream and beat with their fists on the
gates. The human wave has burst against the school. Those
who arrive at the front are crushed against the walls by the
tens of thousands behind. People leap up the gates, work
themselves over the top and drop down on top of us. Blue
helmets try to push back as many as possible.

'Grab this,' yells a Zambian, who is balancing half on the
gutter and half on the top of the gate. A baby is dangling from
his arm. Its eyes have rolled up in its head.

'Now this one!' Another baby hangs from a soldier's hand.
The people outside are trying to save their children by throwing them over the gate. 'Take it. I have to catch them, or
they'll fall to their deaths,' screams a blue helmet in panic.

I grab one after the other: babies, toddlers, screeching and gulping for breath, some unconscious, a few already lifeless and crushed. The Zambian soldiers, holding on to the top of the gate with one hand so as not to fall themselves, clutch tossed-up children from the air and sweep them through to us in a single movement. I grab them and quickly put them down on the ground, anywhere, to be able to catch the next. When we begin to stumble over them, we carry them into the dormitories. We run back and forth with our arms full of children and pile them up until we can scarcely walk without treading on them. The children scream, puke and crawl over each other. One turns out to be dead, crushed, and another can't get its breath, while yet another is hysterically banging her head against the brick wall. Meanwhile, the corrugated iron roof is about to collapse under the weight of the people who've climbed on it.

Back outside, and the little round head of the boy in Bermuda shorts appears suddenly over the top of the gate, mortal terror in his eyes.

'Madame!' he screams to me, but ZamBat soldiers beat on his knuckles with pieces of wood until he lets go and falls into the screaming mass below.

Six hours later and outside the gates all is quiet. The government troops have panicked in the chaos and for several hours have bombarded the crowd with mortars and grenades. All we can do is drag away bodies. With our bare hands, there being no gloves.

The car park has disappeared under a layer of bodies, some weeping and groaning, others dead still. Amongst the motionless piles of people lying by the wall I see several children whose faces are familiar: children whom I personally dragged out of the dormitory into the car park this morning.

A few of our ex-guests are still alive. One lies strangely

curled up between trampled sandbags. I recognize his thread-bare black jacket, far too big for his thin little body. The pupils of his eyes have disappeared into their sockets, but he is still groaning through cracked lips.

'You're not very comfortable, are you?' A Zambian soldier kneels beside the child. He gently straightens the diminutive body: first the head, then the back, then the legs, which seem to be broken. The Zambian arranges them across the body of another little boy: it's the best he can do with the space.

'There, that's better, isn't it?' says the blue helmet cheerfully and wipes some mud from the child's forehead with his sleeve. A stream of blood trickles from the corner of the mouth to the ear. 'You just take it easy here for a while, child. We'll find a doctor or someone to look at you.'

The Zambian stands. 'I know that kid. Hung around for days under our barrier to learn English from us. Nice lad. Full of mischief. I've got two around that age myself.' Silent tears run down his cheeks.

When they were standing, dying of thirst, we could do nothing for them. Now they are lying, dying from their injuries, we can still do nothing for them. The blue helmets separate the dead from the wounded and lay them along the outer wall of the Officers' Mess. They make neat rows of them. That is what they can do. Other blue helmets kneel beside victims and pat their hands to give a bit of comfort. So where do I start then? And what with?

Clumsily, I pat the cheek of someone lying half-buried under a filthy, soggy mattress. 'Hello?' I call. And again.

She's dead, I think. What now?

The next little body looks dead too. I can't make out whether it is a boy or a girl, so deep in the mud is it trampled. Its mouth is open. I see a slight movement of the lips. It is alive.

What now?

The next one is alive too. And then three more. And then two dead. Then a twisted pile in which I can't tell where one person ends and the other begins. I don't even try. Dead or living, piled up or not, I can do nothing for them. Here and there I make things a lot worse by pulling on a broken arm or heaving up people with collapsed lungs.

Another one still alive, but I pretend not to see him. I don't want to go to him, not even to say that a doctor will soon be coming. His lower jaw has been hacked off and I don't want a closer view of the pulp that is left.

For some reason I have no trouble with the scalped head which is not far from him.

'What should you do with this?' asks a blue helmet who is closely studying the open skull.

'I don't know. Maybe keep him upright so his brains don't fall out?' We agree that this is a good idea and the two of us haul the wounded man upright. When we let go he keeps falling, until we get him balanced against the body behind him. He still tilts a bit, but now he stays sitting, dazed but upright. The blue helmet and I look at the result with satisfaction.

'We really should bandage it up, otherwise the dirt will get in,' says the blue helmet.

'Is there a first-aid kit anywhere?'

'Yes, I've already looked in it. Empty, apart from a strip of aspirins.'

There are so many of them and the Zambians keep pulling in new cases, seriously wounded. They drag them into the car park by the wrists, over the bodies of those already there. Then they lay them down, one after the other. Their rows of wounded are just as neat as their rows of dead. Put them down tidily beside the last one, and straight back for more. The

Zambians must have discovered another slaughterhouse out in the crowd. This lot have flesh wounds. So they've been at it with machetes again. That too.

My eyes search for government soldiers. There is a small group next to the bodies by the Officers' Mess. They are standing on top of a pile of rubbish to better survey the car park. One points to the neat rows and giggles. Another examines a basket he has found amongst the dead. Some have slung their rifles across their chests, and are hanging their arms over them. What I am witnessing here is the ultimate abuse of the non-intervention principle contained in the UN Charter. These are the legal authorities.

The metal gates fly open with a clang. Crouched over, heads between their shoulders, seven white men come running in, white coats flapping. They are lugging huge cardboard boxes. For a split-second I think they are angels. Then I spot the MsF logo on their coats.

'Bring in the wounded,' cries one of them. The first boxes are already open. Rolls of bandage appear.

'Help has arrived!' I hear myself shouting. 'Welcome!' A blue helmet and I shake hands in mutual congratulation: the outside world is here, we say to each other. 'The sane world.'

'We're only staying until four o'clock,' says a doctor, tempering our enthusiasm. He is cutting strips of adhesive plaster with little scissors from his box.

I was on my way out to pull wounded free from the dead, but am stopped in my tracks. 'What do you mean, you're leaving at four?'

'Orders from Headquarters,' replies the doctor. 'We must be home before dark. It's too dangerous here.'

It's a quarter past three.

There is no time to argue. The Zambians are already

dragging the first wounded in from the car park, including the man with no jaw. They deposit them all at the doctors' feet. A woman lies on the ground gasping for breath and waiting for treatment, as is a toddler with a machete blow across the cheek. I can see the milk teeth clear through the flesh.

I go outside and haul the first bloody body in soaking rags to its feet. Time is short: 'Come on you, walk, the doctor's here,' I growl impatiently. The body cries and groans as I tug at it, but finally manages to heave itself up and stumble through the gate, leaning heavily on me. Somebody else grabs my leg and hangs on, trying to hitch a lift inside. I shake him off. He's too heavy.

The ZamBat soldiers are bringing in more and more bodies. I run out and grab hold of another, but then have to give up: this one can't stand and I can't lift it. I'll go and help the doctors in the courtyard, then.

The first patients are already sitting in a row against the wall of the Officers' Mess, all stitched up and neatly bandaged. They look gratefully at their bandages and I feel happy. The doctors are working feverishly around me, kneeling beside their patients. With the dazzling white bandages from their boxes, they are miraculously turning muddy flesh, hacked to a purée, back into recognizable human limbs. I hand out adhesive plaster, snip sutures and hold limbs up for bandaging.

Suddenly, somebody announces, 'Four o'clock. We're going!' And the work is literally dropped. Bandages unroll across the courtyard. Zambian soldiers, struggling in with more wounded, tread on them. The jawless man is sitting upright, leaning slightly forward. Someone has put an orange bucket in front of him, into which he spits blood and bits of flesh. No white bandages here: the doctors haven't yet reached him. Nor all those other people on the ground. I am still sitting holding a leg, dumbfounded.

'But what about all these wounded? You told us to bring them all in. And there are piles of them outside,' says a blue helmet amazed.

'We have to go. Sorry.'

'And we've got a few hundred sick children back there in the dormitory.'

'We've seen them. We can't do anything for them.'

'Hurry up!' someone shouts.

'Sorry, but we'll leave you these boxes. Good luck.'

The doctors disappear through the gates. Outside there is gunfire. The doctors come running back in, crouching low.

'Welcome back,' I say.

'Very sarcastic,' retorts one of them, 'but a dead doctor's no use to you either.'

A few of the doctors seize the chance to treat some more wounded. One, who reminds me of the young Alain Delon, just squats against a wall, chewing gum, staring ahead of him. I'm bent over an unconscious woman. For some reason, I think it's a good idea to pour water into her half-open mouth. Alain Delon looks up.

'Turn her on her side. She'll choke like that,' he advises and goes on chewing.

The shooting stops. 'OK. Let's go!' I hear and the doctors run out through the gate once again.

A mortar explodes. They run back. But almost immediately somebody shouts 'It's clear again!'

'Where are they going?' asks Captain Francis who has just arrived.

'Home. They have to be home before dark,' I say.

The Captain's jaw drops so far that I can see his fillings. We watch the doctors slalom between the bodies, jogging towards their Land Rover. We see them stop and bend over. And when they stand up they have found something amongst the bodies: live babies! The deeper they dig, the more they find, and they walk back towards us with their arms full.

'Here. Babies. Just found them,' says a doctor.

'Are you intending to do anything for these babies?' asks Francis.

'We have to go. We're already late,' replies the doctor.

'So the answer is no. Put them back where you found them then. We've already got 400 for whom we can do nothing.'

Silenced, the doctor nods. Then he and his colleagues lay the babies, very carefully, on the ground at our feet.

Only when the Land Rover has disappeared into the chaos of people, does Francis stoop to gather up the dumped infants. He gestures me to do the same. We carry them into the stifling heat of the stinking dormitory.

Hundreds of children. Motionless or vomiting. A few trying to crawl, blood and diarrhoea on their little legs. Francis lies the babies down on a free patch of floor, amongst all the others. He comes out again carrying two dead children.

In the courtyard the doctors have left a shambles of blood-drenched bandages, empty packaging and untreated patients behind them. The patients have been shitting, vomiting and bleeding. Those who have been treated, now sat against the wall, resist all attempts to shift them outside. And we don't have the heart to throw out the untreated. We therefore start raiding the MsF boxes. The blue helmets share out some surgeon's gloves they have found and the Zambian medic discovers, to his visible delight, little bags of intravenous fluid. He immediately sets up some drips on the window frames and connects a few unconscious patients.

I do the rounds of the wounded with half-litre bottles of iodine and large rolls of bandage, to create the illusion that they are receiving the treatment they were promised by being dragged in. Confronting the first gaping wound, I am already hysterical. Sobbing with laughter I bend over shattered heads and half-ripped-off limbs. I can only think of one form of treatment and that is to generously sprinkle with iodine, even inside scalped skulls, and then stick on a bandage. I have never even done a First Aid course. To my astonishment, the patients look grateful and the Zambians ask me if I can help more patients outside. I do, giggling like an idiot, until I run out of bandages and iodine.

The killing goes on throughout the night. So does the rain. When I get up, I really don't know whether I've slept or not.

The rising sun streams over the rim of the mountains. Nothing is moving outside. It is so quiet that I can hear a bird singing on the roof of the school. I install myself on a sandbag. It has been soaked by the rain, but when I notice I don't care. I roll my morning smoke, inhale deeply and enjoy the birdsong. A Zambian passes, raking the ground. He bids me good morning.

'And a very good morning to you,' I say. 'Have you managed to get any sleep?' I look back to where he has passed with his rake. And realize that the Zambians must have worked all through the night. All those dead and wounded who were lying here yesterday, all those pots and pans, mattresses and God knows what else was mashed into the mud, all gone. Miraculous! Maybe I've dreamed the whole thing.

For the first time in my five days in Kibeho, I can see the second Zambian camp, on the other side of the plateau. And only now do I realize that the refugees are still here. It is simply that not one is standing. The Hutus have become one with their possessions in a hideous, sopping wet rubbish tip that stretches to the end of the world.

★

We peer down the mountain road, strewn with bodies, towards the relief troops on the horizon. They are not coming. The roadblocks will remain in place until the afternoon. We understand why: government troops are dragging away all the bodies that can be seen from the road. It is hard to say how many they throw into the cesspits in the valleys. Nor how many disappear into hastily dug mass graves. The fact is that by the time the Red Cross, the UN Force Commander and the President of Rwanda come driving up the road to Kibeho, all that remains are the trampled possessions of the dead.

In the car park the Rwandan President asks Captain Francis, with concern, how many victims he thinks there have been. The Zambian makes a conservative estimate, suggesting 4,000. The figure does not suit the President.

'It sounds to me as if you are exaggerating,' he says coldly. He is inclined to accept the figure of 300 provided by his soldiers.

I discover I'm out of tobacco. So I go and collect my toothbrush from the washroom and climb into a UN car bound for Kigali.

Later I hear that the UN has succeeded in smuggling Captain Francis out of Rwanda alive. With his estimate of 4,000 dead, he was accused of tarnishing the name of Rwanda. Threats had been made on his life.

I leave the UN's Opération Retour to its own devices, go back home to Holland and buy a newspaper.

### Refugees left to rot

Butare, 26 April 1995 – Médecins sans Frontières and Oxfam have publicly criticized the UN's conduct in Kibeho. Why, when the drama had been building up for days, were there only 250 UN soldiers present in Kibeho last weekend? The total

UN force in Rwanda is 6,000. 'They could have sent reinforcements,' said the Director of MsF Holland. 'They did not carry out their task of protecting the population. They did not even support the medical services. Like last year, the UN has shown a tendency to side with the authorities against the people it ought to have been protecting.'

(*de Volkskrant*)

# Epilogue

### Blue helmets leave Rwanda

Kigali, 9 March 1996 – A frustrating mission that failed to prevent genocide or protect refugees, has ended. The UN flag was lowered by Indian, Ghanaian and Malawian peacekeepers in Rwanda to shouts of 'Go home and don't come back.' A Gurkha regimental band kept playing while Rwandans jeered. The Rwanda government declined the UN's proposal to uphold a 1,200-strong UN force in the country. (Reuters)

### UN bankrupt

New York, 2 May 1996 – The United Nations officially went broke today. Only 55 of 185 Member States have paid their 1996 dues in full. 'They're going to shut the heat off,' said an official. 'But it's almost summer anyway.' The UN will borrow $50 million from the peacekeeping budget to allow the organization to operate until August. The UN has already borrowed $1 billion from the peacekeeping fund. (Reuters, AP)

POSTSCRIPT 2001
Soon after the 11 September attacks on New York and Washington, the United States paid $850 million of the back contributions it owed to the United Nations.

# Acknowledgements

The sections of this book which deal with the gorillas in Rwanda and with the insurance detective in Haiti have appeared, in slightly different form, in *de Volkskrant*. A fragment of the account of the Kibeho massacre appeared in *Het Parool*.

An earlier translation of the full story of Kibeho was published in *Granta* magazine.

*Thanks*

Thank you Alex Castanias and Annick van Lookeren Campagne, who were in Rwanda with UN Human Rights, for your friendship.

Thank you Greg Chamberlain, the *Guardian* journalist and Editor-in-Chief of *Haiti Hebdo* (who has spent half a lifetime reporting on Haiti) for years of generous sharing of knowledge and for cheering me on. Whatever my intentions.

Thanks to Iris C. Meyer, Deputy Editor of the *Leiden Journal of International Law*. I was lucky indeed that you could make time to edit my manuscript.

And thank you Mum, Noor, Dirk, Thiba and Neal, the home front. I dare, because you are willing to be my safety net.

A thousand thanks Eliaan Schoonman, Director of the Issues Management Institute in Amsterdam, and effectively Director of this book.

Thank you to everyone at Rozenberg Publishers in Amsterdam, literary agents Jan Michael (Amsterdam) and Toby Eady

(London), and Mary Mount, editor at Penguin (London), for your support.

For the special role Rob Bland has played, I cannot thank him enough. He believed the book deserved to be translated and therefore did it, with an impressive amount of creativity and devotion (and initially at his own expense, too). He then found the book an agent and through the agent, a publisher. With admirable endurance he kept editing and polishing the work up to the deadline and beyond: he cares and worries for the book a great deal, still.

For Rob Bland I wish all his dreams and ambitions come true. Thanks to him, some important ones of mine now have.

*I dedicate this book to Captain Francis Sikaonga from Zambia, Commander of the blue helmet platoon ZamBat, who served the United Nations in the Rwandan refugee camp at Kibeho, and to the eighty ZamBat soldiers who were there with him. Soldiers of peace can't stop people warring. In Kibeho, ZamBat never stopped trying anyway. For that I salute you all.*